DATE			

Jewish Settler Violence

Deviance as Social Reaction

Jewish Settler Violence
Deviance as Social Reaction

David Weisburd
With a Foreword by Albert J. Reiss, Jr.

The Pennsylvania State University Press
University Park and London

R00730 31363

Library of Congress Cataloging-in-Publication Data

Weisburd, David.
    Jewish settler violence : deviance as social
  reaction / David Weisburd ; with a foreword by Albert J. Reiss, Jr.

      p.   cm.
    Bibliography: p.
    Includes index.
    ISBN 0-271-00662-5
    1. Israelis—West Bank. 2. Gush Emunim (Israel) 3. Vigilantes—
West Bank. 4. West Bank—Ethnic relations. I. Title.
DS110.W47W45 1989
956.95'3004—dc19   88–29242
                                                              CIP

Contents

Acknowledgments

This study of deviant social reaction among Jewish settlers in Israel grew out of a series of graduate seminars given by Albert J. Reiss, Jr., of Yale University. He challenged conventional concerns in the sociology of deviance and encouraged research that straddled the boundaries of deviance theory. His own work, which questioned whether social movements or even whole societies may be thought of in terms of deviant labels and deviant identities, sparked my own thinking, just as his support and encouragement allowed me to go off to the Israeli frontier when many others counseled a more conservative course.

My approach to this research was also influenced by a number of other teachers and colleagues. Stanton Wheeler and Paul Burstein provided much support and critical comment, often raising difficult theoretical and empirical questions that less-committed readers would have omitted. Elin Waring of Yale University; Michael Harrison, David Glanz and Gerald Kromer of Bar Ilan University; Chaim Waxman and Myron Aronoff of Rutgers University; and Leon Sheleff of Tel Aviv University also read sections of this work and had important influences on its development. Professor Sheleff deserves special mention, as he provided a crucial Israeli dimension to the development of the project before I came to Israel and helped me to coordinate affiliations with Tel Aviv and Bar Ilan Universities once I arrived to carry out my research.

At various stages I was aided by conscientious and thoughtful research assistants. Of these I owe a special thanks to Vered Vinitski of Bar Ilan University, who gave me a particularly Israeli perspective on the Gush Emunim phenomenon. I also owe much to the help in final preparation of the manuscript provided by Patricia Hardyman, Michael Buerger, Sandra Wright and Ken Coyle of Rutgers University.

My research was supported through fellowships from the National Institute of Mental Health and the Memorial Foundation for Jewish Culture. Preparation of the manuscript was assisted by a stipend from the School of Criminal Justice at Rutgers University. I am very grateful for the generous financial assistance provided by these institutions, but free them of any responsibility for the points of view or opinions that I express in this manuscript.

In bringing this work to press, two colleagues, Freda Adler and Gerhard Mueller, deserve special mention. Their advice about the complex world of publishers and presses, as well as their sincere support for my research, will always be remembered and appreciated.

Finally, I want to express my deepest love and appreciation to my wife Shelly, who gave her intellectual and emotional support to my work during the most difficult of times. Without her encouragement and sacrifice, this study of Jewish settler violence in Israel would never have been completed.

Foreword

The boundaries of domains in a discipline are fluid. New discoveries, enlargement of the empirical terrain, and a reformulation of the questions asked or of explanatory models reshape the contours of a domain. David Weisburd's empirical work on the Gush Emunim settlement movement in Israel reported in this volume reshapes the boundaries of several sociological domains—those of normative order, social control, deviance, and collective behavior. Focusing on Gush Emunim as a normative communal settlement movement viewed as deviant by both the Israeli state and the West Bank Arabs, Weisburd challenges and recasts current theories of value-oriented social movements and the societal reaction theory of deviance. The theory of social control likewise is remolded by explicating settler use of vigilantism as a communal strategy of social control.

The empirical study of value-oriented social movements such as Gush Emunim helps us to rethink conventional societal reaction theory, especially those versions where the State is viewed as the labeling agent. A distinguishing feature of some value-oriented social movements is their challenge not only to the legitimacy of an existing social order, but to the moral claim to State authority. Gush Emunim is such a movement since it threatened both the secular and theocratic divisions of a fragile and divided Israeli state and society by representing historic Jewish claims to sovereignty in the captured territories of the 1967 Israeli-Arab War. Jewish settlers moved into the captured territories, claiming a historic right of all Jews to that land and a religious obligation to do so. Theirs is a special form of deviant social movement, one whose moral claims the State must implicitly recognize as legitimate, but whose means (if not ends) the State must regard as deviant. The power of the social movement lies in its challenge to the

State for not carrying out its moral mandate, a turning of the tables. The State, as well as the movement, becomes a deviant social actor.

Perhaps it is needless to say that there are lessons here for our understanding of the vulnerability of the modern State to particular features of social and political movements. Yet, as Weisburd so nicely demonstrates, the settlers are ultimately constrained in their use of violence, limiting it to the perceived Arab outsiders rather than to the police and military as representatives of the State. Weisburd conjectures that they are constrained from doing so by their social ties and bonds to Israeli society. Others may wonder whether the difference in power of the modern State vis-à-vis any small-scale movement does not account for constraint on both sides. The discretionary use of power may be the better part of valor.

Weisburd's study of the movement adds to our understanding of social control in a number of ways. Deterrence theory is largely built upon rational choice postulates of individual deterrence. Yet what we have in the case of vigilante actions by Israeli settlers toward Arab communities and their residents are attempts to deter collective violence by collective as well as individual punishment. There are distinct limitations to vigilantism as a community-supported strategy of social control when the community is faced with survival in a hostile social environment. Although settlers who experienced victimization by West Bank residents were strongly supportive of vigilante violence, the higher the rate of settlement victimization the less settlers regarded vigilantism an effective means of social control. When victimization becomes chronic, despite the use of collective and violent means of social control, the failures of deterrence to stem victimization become more apparent. Might we conjecture that where violence is collective, the rational choice postulates of conventional deterrence theory are less tenable precisely because it is the collectivity and not the individual experience which is relevant to both those who punish and those who are punished?

This monograph should open our eyes to the much-neglected topic of *collective punishment*. Deterrence literature is built upon individual postulates and the effectiveness of individual punishment. Much of that theory seems inapplicable to the understanding of collective punishments. Vigilantism is a special case of violent collective punishment and Weisburd sheds light upon it as a communal strategy of social control. Yet collective punishment takes many and diverse forms, especially in organizational settings. Often times it is used—and ineffectively so under many circumstances—as a means for detecting individual violators who may be punished. It is commonly used in this way, for example, by school teachers, prison administrators, and military commanders. Yet at other times, it is used with the belief that it is the group that deserves punishment for its collective disobedience or deviance. There is a rich area for theory development and testing on the nature, conditions, and effectiveness of group punishment opened up by this study.

Finally this study makes an important contribution to our understanding of formal and informal social control. The findings of this study place limits upon one of the established propositions in the study of State control—that legal control substitutes for failed informal control systems. For vigilantism as a communal strategy of social control emerged despite considerable exercise of State control over actions against the settlers. What Weisburd's findings suggest is that this informal system of social control arose for two reasons. One was that the settlers were dissatisfied with the government's definitions of what behavior by the West Bank residents required military sanctioning, and, one might add, how they were to be sanctioned. The settlers believed that all harmful behavior, no matter how minor, required immediate and severe reprisal so that they would be protected from future harm. (The government is more discretionary in its use of retaliation.) The other was that the settlers firmly believed that the sanctions would be more effective if the Arab residents understood that Israeli settlers were able to take care of harm against their members. Informal control can be and at times is a substitute for formal control.

This study also amply demonstrates that a solo investigator can effectively use a variety of research methods to shed light upon important theoretical problems. We develop a richer understanding of the limits of societal reaction theory because of the study of a particular case—Gush Emunim—of a value-oriented social movement. We understand far better the relationship between individual and collective actions and experiences because Weisburd used the survey method in a substantial number of settlements to characterize both individuals and settlements. We likewise see the value of the qualitative and quantitative use of historical and cross-sectional comparison. Finally, Weisburd does not shy away from drawing conclusions about what may happen on the West Bank in the months and years ahead, given the findings from this research. I am especially mindful of his insightful statement with its sobering message that for both West Bank Arabs and Israeli settlers "... there is a growing concern with gaining the status of victim and defining their violence as social reaction."

Is that not the course of history?

Albert J. Reiss, Jr.
Yale University

1

Introduction

Scholars have generally recognized few similarities between the behaviors defined as deviant by a community and the reactions brought to sanction and control deviance. In the one case, we have the study of unacceptable conduct, of criminality and outrageous action.[1] In the other, we focus concern upon the organized forces of social control and of social outrage. While these forms of social action are often viewed as intricately linked, interacting in ways that redefine what is considered moral or legal conduct in a society, little similarity is found in their development or social organization.

This study of political deviance and vigilantism among Jewish settlers in Israel grew out of a concern with behavior that violates these traditional boundaries in the study of deviance. What of conduct that fits both our definitions of deviance and those of societal reaction? Such behavior is defined as deviant because it violates the rules and laws of the general society. Yet these deviant acts are themselves a social reaction to deviance: a socially organized attempt to uphold an alternative set of rules and values, or at times to enforce societal norms that appear ignored or forgotten. This scenario is not unknown to social scientists, but it has received little systematic attention.

In this book a very different approach to this problem is taken than that found in other studies. The focus is upon the similarities between certain types of deviant actions and social controls in the larger society. Definitions of deviance of Jewish settlers who themselves advocate or participate in law-violating activities are examined. The social organization of deviant social controls which emerged in settlements established in territories Israel captured in the 1967 Israeli Arab War is described and explained. In this study conventional understandings of deviance are turned on their head. Rather than centering our view of the normative process in the general society, we will examine Jewish settlers who evade and resist the rules and laws of that society.

Limitations of Deviance Theory and Research

The traditional focus in the study of deviance has been upon those traits distinctive or special to the deviant act (Black, 1983). Deviant behavior has, for example, been understood with reference to social disorganization in the community (e.g., Thrasher, 1927), or the differential opportunities for being exposed to and learning delinquent ways (Sutherland and Cressey, 1960). It has been seen to result from breakdowns in community or family bonds (Hirschi, 1969), or imbalances between the organized structural opportunities, or institutional means, to achieve success in a society and the importance given to success as a cultural goal (Merton, 1938). Finally, deviance has been recognized as one possible outcome of social control itself (e.g., Erikson, 1962; Kitsuse, 1962; Becker, 1963), as a result of a system that often works to recruit and amplify deviation (Wilkins, 1965) in the name of justice and corrections. What is common to all of these perspectives is that they clearly distinguish between the nature of deviant behavior and the societal reactions brought for its control.

More than two decades ago scholars began to question whether the clear lines drawn between deviance and social control were consistent with the real world of deviant behavior. They criticized the emphasis placed upon the power of societal reactions and the powerlessness of deviants themselves. Albert Reiss (1966), for example, argued that the picture of deviance presented by sociologists failed to take into account the organizational matrix of much deviant behavior. Alvin Gouldner (1968) suggested that we had created a false image of the deviant actor as a powerless individual victim more sinned against than sinner. Horowitz and Leibowitz (1968) pointed out that obvious comparisons between the rule-breaking of dissidents or "political" criminals and that of more conventional deviants had been for the most part ignored.

While these social scientists called for more research on political and organizational deviance, by the 1980s the dominant perspectives in this area appeared not to have been significantly influenced by their insights. There still was little recognition for the obvious fact that deviants as well as rule-makers may have beliefs and interests which they wish to impose upon the community. As Frances Fox Piven remarked in her presidential address to the Society for the Study of Social Problems:

> When they looked at rule making, they saw a politics of domination, a politics in which some people imposed rules on other people. These rule makers were human actors who, presumably with reflection and purpose, stamped society with their own beliefs and interests, and imposed those beliefs and interests on other people. They also saw the human damage that such imposition could do. What they did not see were the human actors at the other end of rule making who, with reflection and purpose, also try to stamp society with their beliefs and interests by resisting, evading and defying rules imposed on them. (1981:506–7)

In those cases where scholars have turned their attentions to political deviance, they have tended to emphasize the "politics" of deviant behavior rather than similarities between the social organization of rule breaking and rule enforcement. Their primary concern has been with the actual conflicts that define the rules of the general society (e.g., Lauderdale, 1980), or with the ways in which political deviance and its development illustrate the breakdown of consensus views about the nature of deviance (e.g., see Horowitz and Leibowitz, 1968). The predominant themes in this work relate to the politics of rule-making and the effects of political deviance upon society's definitions of rule breaking (see also Kitsuse, 1980; Schur, 1980).

Studies of social movements also examine political deviance. Yet the themes of deviance and criminality occupy a generally insignificant place in this research.[2] In this case, the overriding concern of scholars is with the relationship between strategies of protest and their political outcomes (e.g., Gamson, 1975; Olson, 1965), or with the forces molding the frustrations and emotions that lead to the formation of collective movements (e.g., Smelser, 1962; Gurr, 1970). Accordingly, it is the process which leads to success or failure in the political system or the root causes special to deviant forms of behavior that form the primary focus of inquiry in this research.

Theories of collective movements and political deviance thus help us to understand the development of deviant movements generally, and the challenges they raise both to existing political and social systems. But they rarely address a number of questions that are crucial to our understanding of systems of social reaction and social control. We lack knowledge of the development of ideas about deviance within these groups which are defined as deviant by the larger society.[3] The nature of systems of social reaction in these deviant communities remains unexplored. Finally, these other studies do not provide insight into what distinguishes the reactions of these rule violators from the "societal" reactions used to control deviant behavior.

Some of these questions began to be addressed with the development of "critical" or "radical" criminology in the 1970s (Greenberg, 1981). Paul Walton, for example, studied the American Weathermen movement and concluded that our image of the deviant as a "passive, ineffectual, stigmatized" individual must be altered to take into account the "decision-maker who actively violates the moral and legal codes of society" (1973:18). But the insights of the "new criminology," as it was called by Ian Taylor and his colleagues, were lost in their more general argument that all crime was in fact a form of protest against an oppressive social order (Taylor et al., 1973; Quinney, 1977). Moreover, the view among many prominent advocates of this perspective that criminologists must themselves become involved in political action tended to obscure any special characteristics of collective deviance at the same time that it called into question the objectivity of their research (Michalowski, 1981).

Recently, another group of scholars led by Donald Black has also challenged traditional perspectives that place sharp distinctions between crime and social control (Black, 1983, 1984a, 1984b). Focusing upon the concept of self-help criminal justice, Black argues:

> There is a sense in which conduct regarded as criminal is often quite the opposite. Far from being an intentional violation of a prohibition, much crime is moralistic and involves the pursuit of justice. It is a mode of conflict management, possibly a form of punishment, even capital punishment. Viewed in relation to law, it is self-help. To the degree that it defines or responds to the conduct of someone else—the victim—as deviant, crime is social control. (1984c: 1)

While this "social control" perspective comes closer to addressing the issues raised in this work than earlier theories like the "new criminology," it does not focus systematic attention on the question of collective deviance, but rather challenges whether crime as such may be usefully distinguished from normative behavior (Horowitz, 1987). Indeed the insights of this approach have been applied more directly to such common criminal activities as homicide, rape, robbery, or vandalism (e.g., Black, 1983; Bankston et al., 1985; Scully and Marolla, 1985) than to vigilantism or political violence. While rebellion may fall within this more general theory of criminal social control (e.g., Baumgartner, 1984), it does so not because of its collective social character, but rather as a result of the reactive motivations that underlie such conduct. Similarities between the social organization of deviant social controls and that of societal reaction are not examined by these social control theorists. And thus, they do not address the primary concerns that led to this study.

Deviance as Social Reaction

This examination of collective deviance among Israeli settlers was developed in order to allow a systematic examination of social reactions which are themselves deviant. Like that of more traditional studies of deviance, the focus is upon behavior that violates the rules of conduct of the general society. But, as is illustrated throughout this book, this rule-violating behavior is, at one and the same time, norm- or rule-upholding.[4] The deviant acts we examine are part of a collective, socially organized strategy to control or constrain what subcommunities define as deviant behavior.[5] In this sense, this deviance exists as social reaction: behavior defined as unacceptable in the general society, yet which is organized and developed by a subcommunity to control and sanction behavior that the subcommunity has defined as deviant.

Sociologists have long recognized that there are many divisions and conflicts over the rules governing society. Labeling theory, for example, developed from a concern with the relativity of definitions of deviance and a recognition that different groups in a society may have contrasting views on what constitutes unacceptable behavior (e.g., Becker, 1963). In the "new criminology" these disagreements over the nature of deviant behavior are used to illustrate class conflicts that underlie the deviance process (e.g., Taylor et al., 1973). While the subjective character of definitions of deviance have thus formed an important part of recent perspectives in the study of deviant behavior, in fact little attention has been paid to social reactions in groups which do not represent the dominant values in society.

The study of deviance has remained for the most part the study of social oddities, or as one sociologist has described it— the study of "nuts, sluts and preverts" [sic] (Liazos, 1972).[6] Though there has been a growing concern with white-collar and organizational crime among criminologists (e.g., Katz, 1980; Vaughan, 1983; Geis, 1984; Braithwaite, 1985; Coleman, 1987; Shapiro, 1984; Mann, 1986; Wheeler et al., 1988), with few exceptions (e.g., Johnson and Douglas, 1978; Ermann and Lundman, 1987), such research has generally not informed deviance theory. Moreover, our picture of the white-collar offender does not provide insight into the deviant social reactions that are the focus of this inquiry, but rather fits more comfortably into conventional concerns with criminal motivation and opportunity (e.g., Wheeler and Rothman, 1982; Hagan and Parker, 1985; Coleman, 1987; Weisburd et al., 1987). Deviance that develops from competing definitions of the rules and values which should govern the community and a desire to protect and enforce those values has been generally ignored in the study of deviant behavior.

Deviance may be part of a subcommunity's response to the troubling activities of those who rule a society. It may be used as a strategy to control or punish those who are seen to be managing that society in an incompetent or corrupt way. It may be a response to some serious violation of particular values held by a group within the larger society or even by groups that have their origins and bases in other societies.[7] Deviance of this type often develops as a response to a society's refusal to "live up" to values shared in some form with the deviant group.

We sometimes speak of these rule violators as political or motivational criminals (Schafer, 1971) in order to distinguish them from more "common" law breakers. Yet it is not the motivational nor the political aspects of this deviance that set it apart from the conventional world of deviant behavior. Indeed, labeling these deviants as "motivational criminals" tends to romanticize their objectives (Kooistra, 1985)[8] and fails to emphasize the importance of social organization in their actions. Describing them as political criminals gives them no common attribute beyond the fact that they are labeled as political threats by the society at large (Turk, 1982:114). Clearly, what most distinguishes these deviant acts from other rule violations is that they are a form of social reaction. They represent a socially organized strategy to control what are regarded by the deviants themselves (and the communities or groups which support them) as the "outrageous" or "immoral" actions of the dominant powers in a society.

Deviance may be used as well as a strategy to control what rule violators regard as the offending behavior of other citizens or subcommunities within a society. Whether designed as actions in "lieu of regular justice" (Caughey, 1957:219) or used as a strategy for controlling pariah social groups (see Sederberg, 1978), this vigilantism has had a long and controversial history in American society (Skolnick, 1969; Brown, 1975, 1976; Shotland, 1976; Amann, 1983; Tucker, 1985) and has also been a significant aspect of social control in other countries (e.g., Lebow, 1976; Potholm, 1976; Stone, 1979; Little and Sheffield, 1983; Gitlitz and Rojas, 1983). In contrast to political criminals, vigilantes do not pose a challenge to the normative culture of those who rule society, but rather to their monopoly over definitions of deviance and activities of social control. Their acts, while a violation of law, are generally intended to protect the established order from subversion (Rosenbaum and Sederberg, 1976). Nonetheless, vigilantism is a form of deviant social reaction. Vigilantes violate the laws of the larger society in order to respond to actions their communities define as deviant.

The Focus of Investigation

In this study a subcommunity is examined that has come to live both geographically and socially apart from the larger society from which it is drawn. It is a community which symbolizes an unyielding commitment to the territories that came under Israeli control as a result of the 1967 war. As we will see in later chapters, it is a community that is willing to define the larger society as deviant and use deviant social controls as sanctions. It has also sought to establish its conception of order upon Arab communities, which vastly outnumber Jewish settlements in these regions.

Observations of this community come from a field study of the twenty-two settlements associated with the Gush Emunim settlement movement—Amanah—in the summer of 1981.[9] All but one of these outposts were established in the "Occupied West Bank," as it is generally called in the United States, though the settlers who live in these areas prefer to use the term "Judea and Samaria" when speaking of the region (Figure 1.1).[10] The latter term emphasizes the connection of their settlements to the ancient Land of Israel, the former to the Kingdom of Jordon which sits across the Jordan River on its east bank. One settlement was originally established in the Sinai Peninsula, but it was eventually relocated to the Gaza Strip (also under Israeli control since 1967) after the return of the Sinai to Egypt in 1982. My description of deviant social reaction develops from a detailed field study of these settlements which began in the summer of 1981 and continued until the end of the summer of 1982.

The settlements of Gush Emunim were for the most part struggling young outposts when my observations began. Only two settlements had been established before 1977, and five had been founded within a year of the start of research (Table 1.1). Most settlers still lived in temporary caravan-style housing, though the research was conducted during a period of tremendous growth and expansion in the settlements. Indeed, by the summer of 1982 a number of the settlements had begun developing suburban-style private homes. Of the twenty-two settlements studied, only eight contained 100 or more adult settlers. Seven settlements were composed of fewer than fifty settlers and their children.

Orthodox religious traditions dominated most of these outposts. Seventeen of the settlements were composed exclusively of Orthodox Jews, and these settlements functioned in accordance with Orthodox religious principles. Settlers did no work on the Sabbath, and religious ceremonies and commandments played an important role in their everyday lives. In the three settlements that contained "mixed" populations of religious and nonreligious settlers, there was also public observance of religious traditions, although the nonreligious were not forced to conform in their private lives to Orthodox religious obligations. In two of the Gush Emunim settlements, Jewish Orthodoxy played no official role.

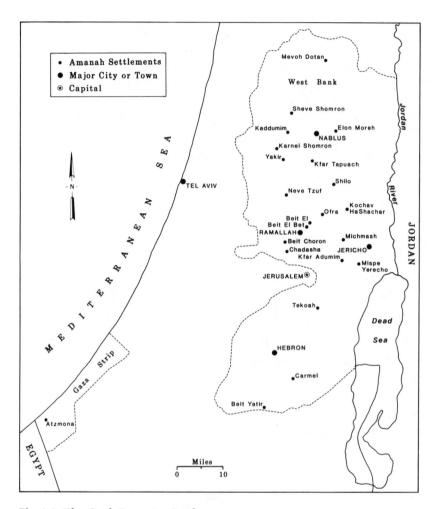

Fig. 1.1 The Gush Emunim Settlements

Table 1.1   Characteristics of the Amanah Settlements (Summer 1982)

Settlement	Date of Founding	Approximate Adult Population	Religious Character	Type of Settlement
Atzmona	March 1979	32	Orthodox	*Moshav Shitufi*
Beit Choron	December 1977	78	Mixed	"Community"
Beit El	November 1977	134	Orthodox	"Community"
Beit El Bet	September 1978	130	Orthodox	"Community"
Beit Yatir	August 1979	36	Orthodox	*Moshav Shitufi*
Carmel	July 1980	32	Orthodox	*Moshav Shitufi*
Chadasha	May 1980	40	Secular	"Community"
Elon Moreh	June 1979	140	Orthodox	"Community"
Kaddumim	December 1975	264	Orthodox	"Community"
Karnei Shomron	December 1977	220	Orthodox	"Community"
Kfar Adumim	September 1979	92	Mixed	"Community"
Kfar Tapuach	July 1978	32	Orthodox	"Community"
Kochav Ha Shachar	September 1980	40	Orthodox	"Community"
Mevoh Dotan	October 1978	42	Secular	"Community"
Michmash	June 1981	52	Orthodox	"Community"
Mispe Yerecho	October 1977	72	Orthodox	"Community"
Neve Tzuf	December 1977	120	Orthodox	"Community"
Ofra	May 1975	200	Orthodox	"Community"
Sheve Shomron	October 1978	94	Orthodox	"Community"
Shilo	February 1978	102	Orthodox	"Community"
Tekoah	October 1977	72	Mixed	"Community"
Yakir	February 1981	80	Orthodox	"Community"

Only three of the outposts studied were organized along traditional Israeli collectivist settlement models.[11] In these cooperative agricultural farms (*Moshav Shitufi*), settlers shared all their work and its income but lived with their families in private dwellings. In the rest of the Gush Emunim outposts a free-enterprise economy was dominant and most settlers commuted to work outside the settlements (Newman, 1985). There was close cooperation between settlers in the areas of social and cultural life, but complete independence in economic activities. Perhaps the major factor distinguishing these communities from other small towns in Israel was their ultimate power to choose and expel members.

The Gush Emunim settlements provided a unique opportunity to study the development of, and variations within, deviant social reaction. The geographic isolation of these outposts

from the rest of Israeli society made them an unusually controlled natural environment where attitudes about deviance
and strategies of deviant social control could be observed and
analyzed. The small size of the individual settlements and
variation in their social composition and development allowed as well for the testing of a number of different hypothe-
ses related to the form and intensity of definitions of deviance
and the social reactions they foster.

While the Gush Emunim settlements thus provided a particularly fruitful site for a study of the forms of deviant social reaction identified here, as with any case study there are important
limitations in what we can hope to learn from our observations.
Some of these limitations derive from the unique political and
social attributes of Israeli society, and these are detailed
throughout this investigation. Others derive from the nature of
the deviant social reactions that have developed in the Gush
Emunim settlements and the wide support that Gush Emunim
has been able to gain in Israeli society (see Sprinzak, 1981;
Lustick, 1987). While the fact that Gush Emunim is not an
"outlaw" organization facilitated the detailed empirical investigation upon which this book is based, it also requires some
caution in comparing deviant social reaction among these Israeli settlers with more strongly sanctioned collective deviance in other societies.

Research Design and Data Collection

To allow for the broadest view of the processes that underlay
the development of deviant social reaction in the Gush Emunim settlements, data were collected using a combination of
research methodologies. At the outset, in-depth open-ended
interviews and intensive field observations were conducted in
each of the twenty-two settlements examined. After these observations were complete, a survey was administered to a
stratified random sample of the settler population.

Perhaps because of the relative isolation of the settlements
from the rest of Israeli society and the fact that they were

overwhelmed by Arab villages and towns in the region, it was generally quite easy to enter the settlement world. While most of the settlements were surrounded by barbed wire fences and guarded twenty-four hours a day, security was reserved for Arabs, not for other Israelis or foreigners who settlers hoped would view the settlements as an integral part of Israeli society.[12]

Settlement field visits sometimes began with introductions to "information" officers. But once it was realized that there was no connection between this research and the news media (which settlers viewed as generally hostile), little interference was given to the research process. Indeed, settlers were generally quite open to questioning and often provided invitations for extending field visits overnight. Travel to the settlements began during the summer of 1981 and field visits continued through the spring of 1982. Observations gained during such visits provided a general view of the social organization and structure of settlement life.

Structured, open-ended interviews conducted during field observations were directed at both "ordinary" settlers and settlement "leaders." Interviews with leaders provided official histories of the settlements and insights into their relationships with the government, Arabs, and other settlement organizations. Particular attention was focused upon conflicts that had developed with the government and Arabs both in the founding and development of these outposts.

While the settlement "secretary" (*Mazkir*) in charge of external affairs was generally interviewed,[13] in some cases, other settlement leaders, for example the head of the "secretarial committee" (the governing body of the settlement—*Mazkirut*), were found to be more knowledgeable or willing sources for settlement history and policy.[14] Often at least two visits to a settlement were needed to conduct these interviews since phone communication was poor and interviews were difficult to schedule.[15]

Structured open-ended interviews conducted with "ordinary" settlers were used to develop a qualitative view of how settlers understood their world and the issues which concerned them most. Thirty-eight interviews were conducted in the sample settlements. The interviews detailed the settlers' involvement in and attitudes toward deviant social reactions directed at the Israeli government and Arabs in the West Bank. Subjects were chosen with the goal of identifying the differing demographic, ideological, and religious groups in the settlements. Settlement founders and newcomers, old and young, men and women, religious and secular, all were interviewed in this process.

In this stage of the research, interviews were also conducted in two illegal settlements (Talmei Yosef and Chotzer Adar) in the soon-to-be-evacuated Sinai Peninsula. Though these were not affiliated officially with Amanah, they were composed primarily of settlers from the Gush Emunim settlements, and their efforts to settle were inspired by the example of other Gush Emunim outposts.

The familiarity with settlement life gained from field observations and interviews both informed and facilitated the survey research carried out in the summer of 1982. While the survey was the most intrusive of the project's data-collection methods, the fact that most settlement leaders and many "ordinary" settlers were already familiar with the research greatly eased the concerns of settlers who were asked to complete the self-administered survey instrument.[16] Moreover, earlier conversations and interviews with settlers allowed for the development of survey items phrased in the vocabulary of Gush Emunim settlers—items likely to gauge accurately their actions and attitudes.

The survey, which included over 100 items, examined social background characteristics of the settlers, their religiosity, their ideology, their attachment to their communities, and their histories of and attitudes toward deviant social reaction. It was administered by two teams of two researchers each completing one settlement in an evening. As a simple random sample of Gush Emunim settlers would have resulted in a large number of responses from the largest settlements and very few from the smaller communities,[17] a stratified selection procedure was used.[18] This allowed for the development of reliable descriptions of each community, thereby making it possible to examine significant variations among them.

In total, some 539 men and women were surveyed out of an estimated population of 2,104 adult settlers.

Unwillingness to participate in the survey was rare,[19] though some settlers chose not to answer certain questions which they found either too personal or too controversial. In two settlements, the survey was hindered by recent events. In Tekoah, the murder of a resident by Arab teenagers from a nearby village and the death of another during the Lebanese War created an atmosphere that made it difficult to approach settlers. In the settlement of Shilo, the police had just used undercover methods to investigate the shooting death of an Arab teenager. The settlers initially thought the survey was another means to collect official information on their behavior.

Some mention should be made of the fact that the survey was conducted during the 1982 war in Lebanon. As many settlers served their army-reserve duties in "Regional Patrols" in the West Bank, and this region was only briefly put on military alert, there was not a large reserve call-up of Gush Emunim settlers. Moreover, the major part of the research was conducted during the early stages of the war, and was therefore not affected by the tremendous soul-searching over the massacres at Sabra and Shatilla and the Lebanese invasion itself that was to come later (see Weissbrod, 1984).[20]

What Was Not Studied

While much effort has thus been made to examine the settlements and settlers of the Gush Emunim movement, no systematic field work has been directed at either the Israeli government or Palestinian Arabs who live near the settlements. The absence of such research is due both to the limitations of this research enterprise and its strategy of inquiry. A study including detailed observations of the Israeli government and West Bank Arabs would have demanded many more resources than were available for this research. But more importantly, such an inquiry would not have significantly altered the picture of deviant social reaction presented here.

The primary concern in this study is to describe and explain how deviant social reactions are developed within the Gush Emunim settlements, and to question how strategies of control are defended and socially organized. It is not the actual success or failure of these strategies, nor the actual "deviance" of those they are directed toward which are most critical in this investigation. Rather, it is the way in which Gush Emunim settlers understand deviance and the way they perceive their social reactions to deviance that form our major concerns. Thus these have as well been the primary focus of systematic investigation.

What Follows

My examination of Jewish settler violence begins with the social and historical roots of the Gush Emunim settlements. While the origins of most conventional deviance are traced to characteristics of individual offenders or the immediate communities in which they live, the origins of deviant social reaction are traced to the normative culture of a broader subcommunity. Thus in chapter 2 a history of deviant social reaction in the Gush Emunim movement and its settlements is presented, and in chapter 3 the relationship between Gush Emunim settlers and the broader Gush Emunim movement is examined. The focus in these chapters is upon the particular religious and nationalist norms which are the source of settler deviance, and the initial strategies of social reaction that they provoked.

In chapter 4 a quite different form of deviant social reaction than that which sparked the founding of the Gush Emunim settlements is examined. Here the concern is with the ways in which settlers defend and understand the development of vigilante actions against neighboring Arab villages and towns. Again, the focus is on collective deviance that has normative roots, though in this case, settlers do not challenge the legitimacy of the larger society's values, but rather its "failure" to exercise effective legal control. Indeed, the legitimacy of settler violence and the forms of illegal coercion settlers relied upon are traced by them to the actions and ideals of Israeli society.

After reviewing the general problem of vigilantism, I question in chapter 5 who in the settlements most strongly supported vigilante actions and was most likely to participate in them. The analysis here is unique in the literature on vigilantism in that a multivariate framework for examining variation in vigilante attitudes and behavior is provided. My findings strongly support a model of deviance as social reaction. The rationalizations that are used to defend vigilantism explain individual settler support for vigilantism. Actual vigilante behavior is linked strongly to the needs and expectations of the Gush Emunim community.

The potential for political violence among Gush Emunim settlers is examined in chapter 6. While the social reactions of settlers have led in the past to comparatively little actual violence, here evidence is provided that points to serious armed resistance if Gush Emunim norms were to be challenged more directly. A striking dissonance is also found between general settler commitment to the normative culture that defines government actions as deviant and support for strategies of violent social control.

The image of deviance presented in this volume provides a stark contrast to dominant themes in the study of rule-violating behavior. Deviant social reaction challenges the neat distinctions between deviance and its control found in most other studies. In chapter 7 the ways in which this perspective has altered our more general understanding of rule violators and rule enforcement are examined.

While observations of settlement life and settler attitudes are used primarily as a means to inform our knowledge of deviance and social control, findings from this study also provide insight into the potential for violence among the settlers who have come to live in these controversial territories. The social control of those who violate laws in the pursuit of a higher law, and who use violence with the confidence of its legitimacy and rationality, are found to present a serious challenge to the powers of conventional policing. In concluding, I examine that challenge as it relates to the control of Gush Emunim settlers.

2

A History of Deviant Social Reaction

The Israeli advance into Syria, Jordan, and Egypt in the 1967 Israeli Arab War provided the spark from which the social reactions of Gush Emunim developed. Much of the enemy territory Israel was to occupy (Figure 2.1) held a special historical or spiritual connection to the Jewish nation. In Jerusalem, Israelis captured the Western Wall of the Temple, the holiest of Jewish shrines, and "reunited" the modern Israeli capital city with the ancient city of David. Within the boundaries of the West Bank captured from Jordan lay much of the link between the Jewish people and the "Land of Israel"—the regions promised to Abraham, Isaac, and Jacob in the Bible, and the focus of Jewish settlement in ancient times.[1] The Golan Heights captured from Syria and the Sinai Peninsula captured from Egypt had fewer associations with the Jewish past, but even there, Jews were not historical strangers.[2]

Between 1949 and 1967, Israel had never seriously challenged the boundaries established during its War for Independence (Gerson, 1978). Traditional ideologies advocating a Jewish presence in all of the regions that were part of the Land of Israel lay dormant (Issac, 1976). But the 1967 victory rekindled discussion and controversy within Israel concerning its national boundaries. Initially there was little dissent from the government's stated desire to exchange most of the captured territories for a peace treaty with Arab states involved in the

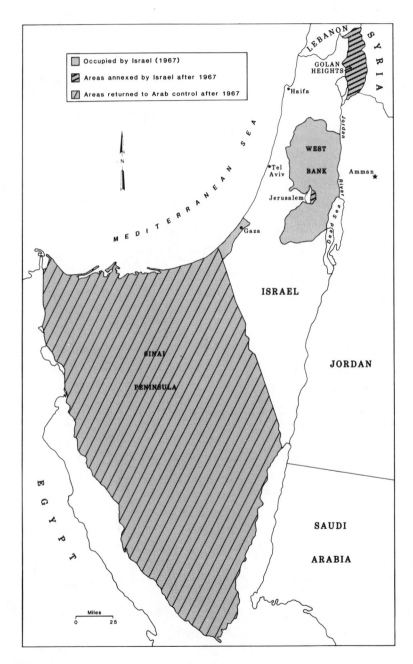

Fig. 2.1 Israel and the Occupied Territories

conflict. Yet shortly after the war, the Israeli consensus established in 1949 began to erode.[3] The war sparked a revival of
traditional religious and secular ideologies for the establishment of Jewish sovereignty in the captured lands. One of the
spearheads of the traditionalist revival was the Gush Emunim
movement.

Although the first Gush Emunim settlements were not established until 1975, they nevertheless emerged from this controversy over the future of the territories captured in 1967. My
history of the Gush Emunim settlements begins with the development of a subcommunity in Israeli society with a special
outlook on the nature of Israel's future and the rules under
which Israel should be governed. From this group's normative
view of the disposition of the captured lands would develop
the deviant social reactions that form the focus of analysis in
this study.

Definitions of Deviance: The Roots of Gush Emunim

The leaders of Gush Emunim were drawn from a new generation of religious Zionist youth in Israel. They were similar to
their parents in religious practice, though at times slightly
more observant of the strictures of Jewish tradition. But their
conception of the role of religion in society was radically different. The older generation, which held the reins of power in
Israel's Zionist National Religious Party (*Mafdal*) in 1967, was
most concerned with areas of public policy directly affecting
religious Israelis, particularly legislation concerning the religious school system, rabbinical academies, and the public observance of religious life by government agencies. In areas not
having a direct effect upon the religious life of the state, the
"older generation" followed the lead of its coalition partners
in Israel's left-wing Labor governments.

The new generation, which came to be associated with the
"youth faction" or "young guard" of the National Religious

Party, saw the role of religion in Israel in a radically different way. They argued that religious legal considerations (*Halachah*) should influence every aspect of public life in Israel (Deshen, 1978, 1982).[4] They saw the *Halachah* as having a direct effect not only on legislation relating to Jewish dietary laws or Sabbath observance, but also upon foreign policy, labor relations, and social welfare.

These young Israelis constituted a generation born after the State of Israel was established. They were for the most part descendants of European Jews, and their most active leaders were a religious elite trained in the newly established religious high schools of Bnai Akiva (the national religious youth movement) and post-high-school rabbinical academies.[5] They represented a new image for religious Israelis. They were unself-conscious of their religiosity, and confident of their full membership in the Jewish nation. They became identified with the "knitted *Kipah*" (skullcap), which was a symbol both of their full commitment to religious orthodoxy and their belief and attachment to religious Zionism. These young Israelis did not see themselves on the periphery of Israeli life. Nor did they see religion as a peripheral enterprise in the modern Jewish state. On the contrary, they felt they could contribute leadership to the entire Jewish nation in Israel (Rubinstein, 1982).

Territorial Compromise and Deviance

At the forefront of this new generation were a number of students who had studied at the Mercaz HaRav *Yeshiva* (rabbinical academy) in Jerusalem. The Dean of the *Yeshiva*, Rabbi Zvi Yehuda Kook, was the son of the first Ashkenazi[6] Chief Rabbi of Palestine, Rabbi Avraham Kook, who was known for his support of Zionism and his good relations with secular Zionist leaders. Rabbi Avraham Kook saw in the modern Zionist movement a sign of the beginning of divine redemption.[7] While the majority of the Orthodox establishment before 1948 criticized the secular Zionist awakening, he argued that the secularists, however unwittingly, were helping to bring about the messianic redemption of the Jewish people. His teachings, which were carried on after his death by his son, Rabbi Zvi Yehuda, took on new meaning with the territorial conquests of the 1967 War.

Even before the West Bank came under Israeli control, Rabbi Zvi Yehuda Kook had placed much emphasis in his sermons upon this region. He spoke of the attachments of the Jewish people to the "whole" Land of Israel, to the cities of Jericho, Hebron, and Shechem, all prominent in the Biblical narratives, but then under Jordanian rule. Immediately before the war, when most Israelis were focused upon the survival of the state within existing boundaries, Rabbi Zvi Yehuda reminded his students that they lived in a "truncated" Land of Israel.

> I was still studying in Mercaz HaRav (on Independence Day, 1967) . . . and Rav Zvi Yehuda spoke. . . . He told of remembrances from the past. He spoke shortly on the building of the State, and then left (to another topic). I was shocked. This was how he spoke: "Where is our Hebron? Where is our Shechem?" This was how he spoke before the Six Day War. No one in the country spoke like this. It was not acceptable. They thought the Land of Israel ended where the State of Israel ended. . . . Part of our education was the sanctity of the Land, the connection between the people and the Land.[8]

Rabbi Kook's sermon evoked tears among many in his large audience, who felt that they had indeed "sinned and forgotten" (Kohn, 1976a).

The question of the future disposition of the territories occupied in the 1967 Six Day War provided the students of Rabbi Kook and the entire younger generation of the national religious movement with a clear-cut case of the new role that Jewish religious law would play in their views on national policy (see Rubinstein, 1982). They looked for Jewish legal opinions to the rabbis of the Bnai Akiva high schools and nationalist rabbinical academies where they had studied, foremost among these the Mercaz HaRav *Yeshiva*. The rulings they received laid the foundations for the deviant social reactions of the Gush Emunim movement.

After the war there was general agreement among Orthodox rabbinical authorities (many of them living outside of Israel) that it was a religious commandment not to relinquish control over the Land of Israel. But the majority argued that the lives of Israel's citizens took precedence over this obligation. In their view, the norm forbidding Israeli withdrawal from the West Bank could not be placed among the small group of *Halachik* proscriptions for which an individual was obligated to accept death rather than transgress (Glick, 1981). Territorial compromise in the West Bank was seen to have strong historical and religious precedents (e.g., see Solovechik, 1975; *Jerusalem Post*, 1980).

In contrast to these opinions, Rabbi Kook, and those national religious rabbis in Israel who followed him, ruled that it was forbidden under any circumstances to relinquish Israeli sovereignty over the West Bank (Odea, 1976; Tal, 1976; Glick, 1981; Weissbrod, 1982). They argued that the sanctity of the land took precedence over the sanctity of human life. For them, the obligation to retain Jewish control over the Land of Israel was a commandment *Ye'Horeg Va'Al Ya'Avor* ("one should rather be killed than transgress"). Explaining the importance of such a decision, Uriel Tal comments:

> This means that Rav Kook sees political sovereignty over Greater Palestine in our time as being so totally fateful, so cosmic in its import, that it resembles the days when Jews were forced to convert and were instructed by *Halachah* to withstand the pressures even giving up their lives rather than transgressing the law. (1976:13)

For Rabbi Kook, the 1967 victory had been a miracle in which the biblical regions of Judea and Samaria were "liberated" from foreign rule. He argued that withdrawal of Israel from this area was forbidden, and would, if carried out, bring about a disruption of the redemptive process begun with the modern Zionist movement (Odea, 1976; Avruch, 1979; Weissbrod, 1982). To relinquish sovereignty over any part of the Land of Israel was, according to his ruling, a transgression of startling proportions. Rabbi Kook had thus provided the younger national religious generation with a normative perspective that allowed them to define the government of Israel as deviant.

Social Reactions to Deviance: The Origins of Gush Emunim and Its Settlements (1973–77)

Prior to the October 1973 war, government actions did not directly transgress the rulings of Rabbi Kook and those nationalist rabbinical leaders who followed him. The government spoke of "territories for peace," but it soon became apparent that there would be no quick political compromise with Arab states in the region. Immediately after the 1967 war, the government annexed the Arab sections of Jerusalem and allowed the reestablishment of Gush Etzion, a settlement in the West Bank that had been destroyed in Israel's War for Independence. By 1973, the government had established forty-five settlements in the Golan Heights, the West Bank, and Northern Sinai. The government did not formally accept ideologies that advocated annexation of the occupied lands. But a policy of annexation that restricted Jewish settlement primarily to areas of sparse Arab settlement had in fact been instituted (Isaac, 1976).

The surprise attack of Arab forces on the Sinai and Golan Heights on *Yom Kippur* (Day of Atonement) in October 1973 sent a shock wave through Israeli society which was to completely alter the prevailing national mood. The sense of self-confidence in Israeli invincibility that developed after the 1967 victory was shattered. Confidence in Israel's political leaders was also shaken (Sprinzak, 1977). A commission of inquiry into the circumstances of the Yom Kippur War laid the blame for Israel's surprise in 1973 on the shoulders of government leaders. It was a period of "demoralization" and "recrimination" in Israeli society (Schnall, 1977). It was also a time when territorial concessions became a real part of government policy, as Israeli leaders prepared for disengagement talks and a Geneva convention for peace.

Before the war a group of friends who had studied at the Mercaz HaRav *Yeshiva* formed a *Garin* (settlement group) for an outpost in Nablus, the largest Arab city in the West Bank. When they returned from their military units after the war, they found a new atmosphere in the country, and circumstances which from their perspective demanded more activity in support of the Land of Israel:

> After the Yom Kippur War there was a very bad atmosphere in the country, and we felt that perhaps it was not enough (now) for us to be active in building a settlement in Hebron, or to go to a (new) settlement in Shechem (Nablus). There was a need to do something more general, something that would wake up the nation. Not only one more point. . . . In discussions after the War . . . we felt that there must be a change. . . . We were a group of friends. . . . And in the end this is how Gush Emunim was born.

After several small meetings, a few hundred people came to a founding convention in the settlement of Kfar Etzion (in the Gush Etzion region) on February 7, 1974. They took on the name *Gush Emunim BeMafdal*—the Block of the Faithful in the National Religious Party (NRP)—as they initially intended that they would comprise a pressure group within the NRP. The leaders of the convention were drawn primarily from the followers of Rabbi Kook, among them Beni Katzover and Menachem Felix from the *Garin* for Nablus, Chanan Porat from Gush Etzion, Rabbi Moshe Levinger, the leader of the Kiryat Arba group that settled in Hebron in 1968,[9] Rabbi Waldman, Rabbi Yochanan Fried, and Rabbi Chaim Druckman, one of the leaders of the national religious youth movement—Bnai Akiva. The group chose from the outset not to establish any formal membership, and the leadership by consensus was drawn from the convention's founding fathers.

Settlement as a Strategy of Social Control

In the spring of 1974, Gush Emunim became more than just a pressure group within the National Religious Party. In May, the group gave its support to leaders of the primarily secular "Whole Land of Israel Movement"[10] in their hunger strike to protest possible disengagement treaties on the Golan Heights and Sinai Peninsula. More important in terms of the future actions of the movement was its decision to provide settlers for an unauthorized outpost sponsored by Kibbutz Meron Ha Golan in the town of Kunitra.

Members of the nonreligious Kibbutz, who feared the town would be returned to Syrian rule as a result of the disengagement accords, had turned to collective settlements in northern Israel for recruits for the site without success. Finally, they turned to Gush Emunim, and when on May 31 a disengagement agreement was signed, in a bunker in Kunitra there was a Gush Emunim-supported "settlement"—Keshet. This experience was to set a precedent for illegal settlement in support of the movement's territorial norms (Rubinstein, 1982:52). Settlement, in the eyes of Gush Emunim's leaders, would, as it had in the past, set the boundaries of the Jewish commonwealth (Avruch, 1979).

After the disengagement accords of May 1974, fears among Gush Emunim leaders that the diplomacy of Henry Kissinger would lead to accords not only on the Golan Heights and Sinai Peninsula, but also on the West Bank, led to an acceleration of Gush Emunim activities. Much of the heartland of this area, precisely those regions with the clearest links to biblical Israel, had been placed off-limits to Jewish settlement. According to the Allon Plan, which provided the general guidelines for government settlement policy, these densely populated mountainous areas (Figure 2.2) would not become integrated into the Jewish state (Ben Zadok, 1985). The Labor government focused settlement efforts instead in less populated regions along the Jordan Rift. This fact underscored the fears of Gush Emunim's leaders that Judea and Samaria would be returned to Arab control in the context of a disengagement accord or general peace treaty.

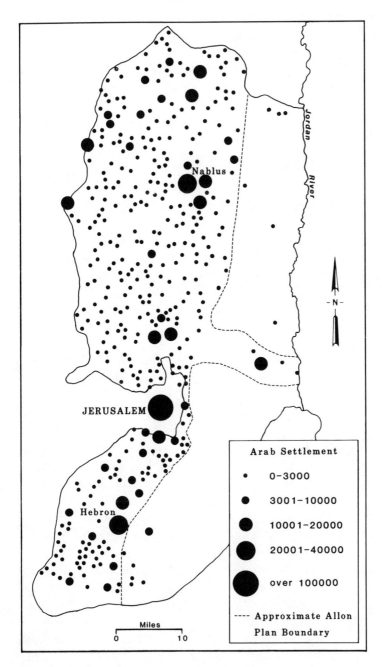

Fig. 2.2 Arab Settlement on the West Bank

In June 1974, the first large-scale illegal settlement attempt sponsored by Gush Emunim in the West Bank was carried out outside Nablus. The settlement attempt by the Elon Moreh settlement group was forcibly prevented by the Israeli army. The settlement move, however, attracted support not only from religious elements but also from secular Israelis of varying political backgrounds. For the Gush Emunim leadership, these events showed that their message crossed party lines and their actions would be supported by many non-Orthodox Jews. At the same time, they saw their struggle within the NRP becoming "rather hopeless," and thus Gush Emunim became independent of the National Religious Party (Kohn, 1976b).

In the summer of 1974, there were further unsuccessful settlement attempts by the Elon Moreh group. In October, Gush Emunim sponsored "Operation Go-Around" (Sprinzak, 1981), in which 2,000 people spread across the West Bank to sites the movement proposed for settlements. On October 20, a rally of over 12,000 people was organized in Tel Aviv against restrictions on Jewish settlement of the West Bank. Participants included not only Gush Emunim activists and opposition members of Parliament such as Ariel Sharon, but also a number of supporters of the ruling Labor party (see Honig, 1974).

In the beginning of March (1975), another settlement attempt of the Elon Moreh *Garin* led to "violent clashes" between soldiers and settlers. Though this event and other similar conflicts led to serious injuries in only isolated cases, the scenes of Jews fighting Jews graphically portrayed on television and in the press were traumatic ones for the young nation and the settlers (*Jerusalem Post*, 1975). Also in March, during the intermediate days of the Passover holiday, 20,000 Israelis participated in a Gush Emunim-sponsored march to Sebastia near Nablus, the site of the biblical city of Shechem (Brilliant, 1975a). Throughout this period, Gush Emunim organized smaller protests against the government and the diplomatic activities of Henry Kissinger.

Meanwhile, other settlement groups were being organized by Gush Emunim. Protest actions did not obscure the movement's primary concern with actual settlement on the West Bank as a means of ensuring Jewish sovereignty in the region (Sprinzak, 1981). By January 1975, there were six *Garinim* (settlement nuclei). These included Elon Moreh, Yerecho, Maale Adumim, Maarav HaShomron, Shilo, and Tekoah (Gush Emunim, 1975). Though the first illegal settlement attempts were brought by the Elon Moreh group, other *Garinim*, notably Yerecho, Shilo, and Maale Adumim also staged independent settlement bids.

The first Gush Emunim settlement in the West Bank was established without conflict, though also without government authorization, in April 1975:

> A group of Gush Emunim members wanted to build a settlement in the Shilo region. And they had many contacts with the government and exhausted every possible means without finding a way to build (a settlement) in these areas. . . . And then someone got an idea. There was in the region, not far away, a military base. (The idea) was to approach one of the contractors (for the base) to get work. And then in the bargain (we would argue) that to begin work (at the site) and also to go back and forth (to the city) was impossible. . . . And in truth we met a Jerusalem contractor that received work (at the military base) and we contracted (with the Jerusalem contractor) to do the fence work at the base. . . . And this is how it (the settlement) began. . . . In the beginning we traveled daily from Jerusalem to the region to work (as a sub-contractor).

The settlers saw an abandoned Jordanian army barracks on their daily commute back and forth from the base. They decided to try to get permission to use the barracks as temporary quarters while they worked. Eventually, they were allowed to use the barracks during the day, but not for overnight stays. By that time, the group was already getting impatient for the start of a settlement. It was winter and their fence work at the base "was not exactly their profession":

> And thus we decided that one day after work with all of the settlement group participating, we would come to

sleep in that place (the army barracks). . . . We chose that place because there were buildings and we could get water and electricity. There was a possibility to begin a settlement in an unconventional way. . . . We called the Army and told them we were there. At the beginning there was an order to return us to Jerusalem. . . . In the morning seven advisors of Rabin (then Prime Minister) came. . . . Their answer was that they would not prevent the people that worked in the military base from sleeping here. This is exactly the event we had been waiting for—this began our settlement, which was not called a settlement by the newspapers and the government at that time. They called it a work camp, because of the issue of work there. We didn't receive support from the government or the Jewish Agency or anything like that—only from . . . individuals. And that in truth, (was how) we began the settlement. . . . And all different types of people came to help.

The settlement which called itself Ofra began with only five families and some single people. By the summer, the site had twenty-three families. The settlement bid had been a success. The first settlement had been built in Samaria, and settlers believed that they had begun the task of preventing territorial compromise in the West Bank. For them, settlement was itself a strategy of social control:

The purpose was to build a Jewish settlement here in Samaria—the first settlement in Samaria in the area between Jerusalem and Jenin: with the assumption that this land belongs to the nation of Israel. And if settlements are not built here, then there is a weaker chance that this land will remain in the hands of Israel.

The Kaddum Compromise

In November 1975, a series of settlement attempts similar to those of October 1974 began. Two of these were successful in establishing West Bank outposts. The settlement group for

Maale Adumim went up to an "industrial" site already approved by the government in the Judean Hills east of Jerusalem, though their move came three weeks before the planned date for the settlement's establishment. The group was not evicted, but it was not officially recognized until the Begin government came to power. Of much more consequence for the Gush Emunim movement and its settlements was the eighth settlement attempt or *Aliyah* (literally "going up"), as settlers described it (using a phrase ordinarily applied to immigration to Israel), of the Elon Moreh *Garin*.

For this group, as for other Gush Emunim settlers, the government's refusal to allow *Aliyah* to certain areas of the West Bank was itself a serious transgression. They saw no distinction between attempts to settle modern Palestine before the state's founding and their efforts in Judea and Samaria. Thus, for the settlers, the government's position constituted a modern "White Paper" against the Jewish people, similar in its content to the British White Papers of the 1930s which limited Jewish immigration to Palestine and resulted in sometimes violent resistance to British rule (Bell, 1977).

> In the Labor government the concept (for settlement) was the Allon Plan. And all of Samaria was not a part of that conception. . . . Because of this they (the Labor government) were against action in this region. This was the "fact" part of the struggle. The second side was: If the government does not want to (settle), then don't bother us when we do it. This was the period of struggle. . . . There was a law of the army in this region, that it was forbidden for a Jew to remain 24 hours without permission. . . . And we complained that this is a "White Paper" against the Jews in the State of Israel. To come and define that it's forbidden for a Jew to remain on the land more than 24 hours according to the law—this is in action a "White Paper." The government has defined "districts" (where Jews may not settle) in the Land of Israel. And thus on this basis there grew some settlement "experiences."
>
> The eighth experience, in the way of it, was almost

the same as the earlier ones. There was not anything special, except that it was during Hannukah (and) we learned from the earlier experiences that there should be more people involved in the event. That is to say, the *Garin* as a settlement group was not large—at that time . . . perhaps there were 18 families ready to live at the settlement. (But) in the area all of the time there were thousands.

Twenty-five thousand Gush Emunim supporters came to the settlement site at Masudiya near Nablus (see Brilliant, 1975b). They were drawn from a variety of backgrounds, both religious and nonreligious, though the young generation of national religious Jews predominated. The group was joined by Jewish leaders from outside the country who were in Israel to participate in the Jerusalem Conference of Jewish Solidarity with the State of Israel. On December 4, with 600 supporters remaining, the group placed *Mezuzot* on the doorposts of their "sheds" (Brilliant, 1975c). Six delegates from the Jewish conference participated in the ceremony—one which is performed according to Jewish law only on permanent dwellings. Among the visitors was the Chief Rabbi of South Africa and the president of the Orthodox Rabbinical Council of America.

While the government had acted quickly to forcibly uproot previous settlement attempts, it did not move against the settlers in Samaria through December 7. The settlers indicated that they would forcibly resist soldiers who tried to evict them. The combination of the large number of "settlers" and a desire to avoid a major conflict while the diaspora Jewish conference in Jerusalem was in session were most probably responsible for the government's reluctance to act (Brilliant, 1975b). On December 8, after negotiations had broken down, 1,250 Gush Emunim supporters waited at Masudiya for the government to forcibly evict them. However, in order to avoid a clash, the government offered a compromise solution whereby the Elon Moreh *Garin* would settle temporarily in a military camp at Kaddum in Samaria (Brilliant, 1975d).

For settlers, the establishment of Elon Moreh at Camp Kaddum constituted a miraculous event. It came on the eighth day of the eighth settlement attempt on a holiday commemorating a miracle which lasted eight days. Yet government leaders, who fought among themselves over the compromise, did not formally recognize the settlement, and it remained unauthorized throughout the period of Labor Party rule.

The Changing National Mood

Rabbi Levinger, a well-known Gush Emunim leader, promised, after the Kaddum compromise, that "we will have to call this group again" if the government did not change its settlement policies (Brilliant, 1975d). In fact, though new settlements were not established in the months following the events at Masudiya, Gush Emunim did not stage any new illegal settlement actions. This may be attributed, in part, to the continuing political struggle over the unrecognized settlements of Kaddumim, Ofra, and, to a lesser extent, Maale Adumim, as Gush Emunim settlers tried to build up the fledgling new settlements (without government help), and "dovish" groups in the government attempted to have them removed or relocated. The change in tactics may also be attributed to the growing support for Gush Emunim's settlement efforts within Israel's traditional political parties.

In April 1976, when "doves" in the government cabinet threatened to call for the eviction of the Kaddum settlers, Menachem Begin (then head of the opposition) claimed that he would call a special session of the *Knesset* (Parliament) to defeat the move (Landau, 1976). Begin, soon to become Prime Minister, asserted that he had the support of the majority of the *Knesset* against the eviction of the group. His majority included fifteen members of the religious parties (many of them part of the coalition government), and seven Labor members of Parliament. Strong support for Gush Emunim's West Bank settlers also came from Labor settlement groups, who at the Ein Vered Conference voiced strong opposition to their removal (*Jerusalem Post*, 1976). Gush Emunim formed a number of new settlement "nuclei" during this period, and with their new support they acted to exert pressure upon the government to establish these outposts (Sprinzak, 1981).

By the spring of 1977, the government had approved settlements at the Gush Emunim sites of Tekoah, Beit Choron,
Ma'sha (later Elkana), and Givon. Settlers feared, though, that
the government would not in fact act upon their promises
unless pressured. At Ma'sha, settlers went up to the site without government approval in February and were removed to an
army camp nearby. In the beginning of May, they were allowed into the actual settlement site. At Givon, a group of
non-Orthodox Gush Emunim settlers moved into a temporary
settlement shortly before the Likud election victory in May.
Even though the settlement was established with government
help, Givon settlers viewed their action as an act of "political
war"—dependent on their moving immediately after government authorization was granted.

Gush Emunim continued to stage mass rallies of support for
settlement. In April 1976, during the intermediate days of
Passover, 20,000 to 35,000 people participated in a two-day
march in the West Bank which began at Beit El and ended near
Jericho. A mass rally of some 30,000 to 40,000 people was held
as well during the intermediate days of Passover in 1977. In
March 1976, the Jericho group staged another unsuccessful
settlement bid, and in August 1976, Gush Emunim supported
an unsuccessful attempt by Kiryat Arba settlers to occupy the
abondoned Hadassah building in the city of Hebron.

By May 1977, when Likud won a surprise victory in the
Knesset elections, Gush Emunim supporters saw themselves
as a major reason for the defeat of the Labor coalition (which
had been in power since the state's founding). But more important from our perspective, the period between 1973 and 1977
established for the supporters of Gush Emunim the principle
that settlement could be used as a strategy of social control, as a
means of preventing territorial compromise on the West Bank.

The ruling of Rabbi Kook that withdrawal from the West
Bank was forbidden placed the question of the future of this
region and Jewish settlement in it above Israeli law (Weissbrod,
1982; Rubinstein, 1982). This was not politics as usual. Gush
Emunim's leaders had adopted the language of deviance—of
transgression and unacceptable action, not of compromise and
political debate. For them, discussion of the future of the West

Bank was not subject to the same rules that governed other decisions in Israeli life (Sprinzak, 1981). As Rabbi Moshe Levinger remarked:

> The Jewish national renaissance is more important than democracy. Democracy can no more vote away Zionism, aliyah, settlement, than it can vote that people should stop breathing or speaking. The fate of *Eretz Yisrael* (the Land of Israel) and a free and whole Jewish life in it are not subject to a majority vote. (Kohn, 1976b)

The question of settlement in the entire Land of Israel lay outside the boundaries of acceptable political debate:

> If the government was to make a law that there is to be no *Aliyah* . . . I don't know what I would do. But it is a type of law which no government has a "right" to enact. That is to say, according to the law (of the country), theoretically speaking, the government can do it. . . . But the government does not have the "right" to make a law which says that a Jew cannot make *Aliyah*. And no government has the authority or right to say that a Jew cannot live in all of the parts of the Land of Israel.

Law-violating actions were thus seen by Gush Emunim settlers and activists as a legitimate strategy to control what they defined as governmental deviance. Illegal settlement was a social reaction of the Gush Emunim community. Its purpose was to prevent the government from transgressing Gush Emunim norms concerning the Land of Israel.

Gush Emunim Under Likud Rule: The Consolidation of Settlement

One of Menachem Begin's first acts after his victory in the *Knesset* elections of May 1977, even before his government assumed power, was to go to the unrecognized settlement of Elon Moreh at Kaddum. There he participated in the dedication of a synagogue and danced with the *Torah*.[11] He promised the ecstatic Gush Emunim settlers that there would be many more Elon Morehs "in the land of liberated Israel" (Farrell, 1977a). Already in early June, Gush Emunim was planning for ten new settlements to be established in the West Bank (*Jerusalem Post*, 1977a). There was at that time no reason for them to doubt the success of their plans. Prime Minister Begin had campaigned on the platform that "Judea and Samaria" were "liberated," not "occupied" territories, which must eventually be annexed by Israel.

Following up on campaign promises, Begin gave official government approval to the unrecognized settlements of Ofra, Kaddumim, and Maale Adumim in July 1977. But Begin's move brought a strong American response of condemnation from President Carter (Farrell, 1977b), who believed that settlement in the occupied territories was both illegal and an impediment to peace. This set the stage for a series of confrontations over settlement between the American government and Israel. In turn, the settlers' initial euphoria turned to distrust as they saw American pressures and Israeli coalition politics[12] leading to an impasse on the settlement question. By September, not a single Gush Emunim settlement had been built by the new government. Gush Emunim settlers felt betrayed: "We thought that after all of his talking, Menachem Begin would put up dozens and dozens of settlements immediately, if not sooner . . . and our help was no longer that important. . . . We found that between his talking and his actual deeds in those years (there) was a very big difference."

Illegal Settlement Is Renewed

Initially, Gush Emunim leaders heeded a public plea by Rabbi Kook that they cooperate with the new government, which he said was "granted by the grace of God and the belief of our people" (*Jerusalem Post*, 1977b). But by the end of September, they were dissatisfied with the results of their meetings with the Prime Minister and decided to move on their own. Their threatened actions were different from earlier illegal settlement moves both in the large number of "actual"[13] settlers involved (2,500), and the fact that the government in principle was sympathetic to their goals. Two settlement groups (Yerecho and Dotan) set out before any official decision was reached by the Gush Emunim leaders in Jerusalem. They were forcibly removed by government troops. Shortly afterward, before the other ten groups were to begin their settlement actions, the Gush leaders accepted a government plan for the establishment of civilian settlements as part of military bases, a plan that they had rejected in principle earlier (Brilliant, 1977a).

Because military settlements were legal in occupied territories under the rules of the Geneva Convention, Begin hoped he could avoid American condemnation by establishing the sites in army camps. The plan was for settlers to be called up for military reserve duty for an indefinite period of time, and for their wives and families to follow them shortly afterwards. Under the agreement, six military camps were to be opened to the settlement groups in the following three months. While not happy with the proposal, Gush leaders argued that they did not want to endanger the Begin government's narrow coalition majority by causing a major confrontation between the army and settlers—a possibility which became apparent after the settlement groups of Yerecho and Dotan had been stopped by the army. For the Dotan group itself, the settlement action was seen as a success, prompting the government's decision for their settlement to be established.

> It was a time when Gush Emunim prepared 12 settlement groups to go up (to the sites) on *Sukkot* (Feast of Tabernacles). And they didn't allow us to go up. So our men came at night to Sanur . . . and the army came and removed them. (Was there violence?) No, there wasn't violence. It was tactical and it was elegant. But it was a fact that we came to the site and they would not allow us to settle. We built a tent and put up an (Israeli) flag,

and then the army came and removed us. And then very fast, after two weeks, we received a green light. They said we could go up.

In the next three months, six settlement groups were, in fact, placed in army camps. These included Beit El, Karnei Shomron, and Neve Tzuf in the Samarian hills, Dotan in the north of the West Bank near Jenin, Beit Choron on the Latrun-Ramala road, Mispe Yerecho on the road between Jericho and Jerusalem, and Tekoah, east of Gush Etzion. The settlers were offered jobs at the military bases, but were not made military personnel. They signed papers giving them the status of persons "employed in a mission on behalf of the army," thus making them part of the garrison force, and avoiding, in the government's view, international pressure against civilian settlements in the West Bank (Brilliant, 1977b). At the same time, it was clear to settlers that they were creating civilian settlements and not acting as civilian support at military bases. In this they were supported by the head of the ministerial settlement committee, Ariel Sharon, who argued at the end of October that the "militarization" of Gush Emunim settlers should not be taken too literally (Brilliant, 1977c).

Conditions in the camps were for the most part primitive. Settlers, though hoping to form noncooperative communities in the future, were forced to live a cooperative life-style. There were no private kitchens, and often no private toilets. The settlement families, many of which were composed of five or six members, lived in small caravan-style (trailer) housing. But for the settlers, there was no alternative: "If the people here would not have been ready to live in such conditions, then this settlement would not exist . . . and it's the same at every other settlement. It was more . . . the people here just caught the government by the neck, and thus got what they had."

The Shock of Peace Proposals

In the winter of 1977, Anwar Sadat's dramatic journey to Jerusalem and subsequent negotiations over an Egyptian-Israeli peace treaty took Israel and Gush Emunim by surprise. In December 1977 when the Begin government adopted a peace proposal calling for "autonomy" in the West Bank and a withdrawal from most of the Sinai, Begin changed from a "hero" of the Gush Emunim movement to a "traitor" almost overnight (Rubinstein, 1982). But immediately following the December peace moves, the government established the Karnei Shomron settlement and approved two other sites in the West Bank—Harris and Shilo (Brilliant, 1979). In early January, Begin announced plans for large-scale settlement in Judea and Samaria.

In February, the settlement group of Shilo decided to act on its own after government promises for settlement were not fulfilled:

> Shilo did not have an army base. On the other hand, before he left (to meet with President Carter) Mr. Begin promised us (through intermediaries) he would put up Shilo. And when he came back he was in a dilemma. . . . So he checked the possibility of putting an army base up. . . . The answer was no. . . . Because of that they had to solve the situation another way. And the solution was: the Hague Convention allows for an occupying force to have an archaeological dig.
>
> So we were in a situation where we were offered by the government to come here as an archaeological dig. And even then it was not easy until they found a university to do it, and they did find finally—Tel Aviv University. And then the minister of education announced it on the radio. The next morning, Meir Peil, one of the members of the board of Tel Aviv University, convinced all of the other members that this was for political reasons.
>
> Meanwhile we had been told that we could come. And then we came and there was no dig. We were called . . . everything under the sun. But in actuality we were doing what the government told us to do. They were eight families (who went up) that were basically adopted by the army.[14] And that was it. And the government said: You're not really here.

The settlement caused an international incident as President Carter claimed that Prime Minister Begin had promised there would be no more settlements in the occupied areas. The Begin government's refusal to forcibly remove the settlers angered the Americans. Yet the government did not recognize nor support the Shilo group, perhaps hoping the settlers would retreat on their own.

In the shock of recent peace moves, and while improving conditions in the score of Gush Emunim settlements already established, the movement remained relatively quiet throughout the spring months. Gush Emunim sponsored a number of small protests but avoided any major settlement moves. In July, it presented a settlement plan to the government which called for 100,000 settlers in Judea and Samaria during the coming three years, and 750,000 by the turn of the century. The group also requested that the government begin developing permanent sites for the already established settlements, which were still in temporary camps or military outposts. In the summer, the government established two more Gush Emunim settlements: Sheve Shomron at an army base outside Nablus, and Kfar Tapuach on the Ramala-Nablus road.

The Camp David Accords

In September (1978), when news of the Egyptian-Israeli agreements reached Camp David (which called for a return of the Sinai Peninsula to Egypt and "autonomy" for Arabs in the West Bank), a new period of crisis began for Gush Emunim. The proposed Sinai accord brought into stark reality the possibility of a large-scale withdrawal from the West Bank. Settlers were confused, as were others, about the meaning of autonomy, but feared that it would lead to Arab control of the area. Word of a three-month settlement freeze agreed upon at Camp David only reinforced their fears that territorial compromise on the West Bank would become a part of the peace process.

By the time of the Camp David negotiations, Gush Emunim settlers had begun to occupy the central stage in activities associated with the larger movement. In 1978 the settlement "secretariat" of Gush Emunim, which had been established early in the movement's history, became Amanah—the settlement organization of Gush Emunim. The need for the organization, as well as the developing importance of settlements within the Gush Emunim movement, grew from the expanding population of actual settlements and settlers in the West Bank. Some official settlement organization, like that of other Israeli settlement federations, was needed to coordinate activities with the government for the development of established outposts, to screen potential settlers, and to organize new settlement *Garinim.* Importantly, while establishing Amanah to gather government assistance for settlement, the settlers did not lose sight of their commitment to the territorial norms of the Gush Emunim movement.

On September 18, when the news of the signing of the accords at Camp David reached Israel, the original settlement group of Elon Moreh (which had retained its independent identity within Kaddumim) decided that it was time to establish, as they had always intended, a settlement in Nablus:

> And then with the announcement of the autonomy plans and the agreements after Camp David—we understood that now it was more serious and more urgent than before. And the same day on the night of the signing of the Camp David accords we decided to make our *Aliyah* (to establish the settlement).

Two hundred settlers camped on Mount Hawara, south of Nablus (Rabinowitz, 1978a). On September 21, the third day of their attempt, "hundreds" of soldiers came to remove them (*Jerusalem Post*, 1978). During the eviction, there were outbreaks of fisticuffs and kicking, with some injuries among both settlers and soldiers. While most of the injuries were minor, with only one settler requiring hospitalization, the event marked the first time that the Begin government had carried out a serious forcible eviction of settlers.[15] For their part, Gush Emunim activists promised to set up settlements each night until the government recanted on its Camp David pledge not to establish new outposts on the West Bank for three months.

A series of settlement bids and protests were begun by other Gush Emunim settlement groups. Though these demanded much attention by the military, which argued that the experience of Jew fighting Jew was traumatic for the soldiers (Goodman, 1978), they led to little violence and, indeed, little public support outside the settlements. At the end of September, the *Knesset* voted overwhelmingly to approve the Camp David accords. A protest organized by Gush Emunim shortly afterwards outside the *Knesset*, which organizers hoped would attract 30,000 people, was attended by fewer than 1,500 (Rabinowitz, 1978b).

The ratification of the Camp David accords temporarily "paralyzed" Gush Emunim settlers and activists (Sprinzak, 1981). But in December, the group once again threatened illegal settlement if the Begin government refused to establish new outposts after the three-month freeze promised at Camp David ended. On December 27, a series of settlement bids began. While the government prevented most of the settlers from reaching or remaining at their sites, the settlement of Kfar Adumim marks its establishment from this time:

> This (settlement) was already part of the plan of Ariel Sharon before Camp David. . . . After Camp David they promised Carter not to build settlements for 90 days in the Land of Israel—the freeze. When 91 days ended, we traveled to the Arab below (guarding the site) . . . and we jailed him all night. After three days there remained for us a settlement.

Begin promised that there would be more settlements, but at a time and tempo of the government's choosing. In regard to the Elon Moreh group, which had set up a "settlement" on the highway to Nablus (where they were stopped by the army, but not evicted), Begin remarked:

> I want you to believe me that my heart pains me when I think of the Gush members out on the highway near Kaddum in this cold and rain. . . . I want you to urge

them to give up their demonstration. Let them put their proposals forward. But they cannot dictate to the government. (Wallfish, 1979a)

On January 7, the Elon Moreh settlers returned home to Kaddumim after receiving assurances that a settlement outside Nablus would be recognized within three months.

From January (1979), it became apparent that Begin's commitment to Gush Emunim and settlement in the West Bank remained strong. Gush Emunim pressed the government for the approval of new outposts but refrained from illegal actions in the region. Gush Emunim settlers were nevertheless involved in demonstrations and settlement actions against the proposed withdrawal from Sinai. On March 19, when Begin was in Washington for the signing of the peace treaty with Egypt, sixty settlers established the illegal Gush Emunim settlement of Atzmona in the Northern Sinai: "After Camp David, Atzmona was created (as if to say) 'you go to uproot settlements (in the Sinai) and we will build a settlement.' " While the army sealed off the roads leading to the settlement, the outpost was not removed and, in fact, remained without government approval until it was relocated in the Gaza strip after the withdrawal was completed.

By the end of March, the government had quietly changed the status of Gush Emunim's "military outposts" in the West Bank to civilian settlements, and formed Jewish Regional Councils that gave settlements an administrative status independent of the autonomy framework. In April, the government formally recognized the settlement of Shilo, established a year earlier, and approved the establishment of an Elon Moreh site on the outskirts of Nablus. Ezer Weizman writes that Begin and his supporters were "alarmed" by the peace treaty they had just concluded, and thus they "eroded their achievement (at Camp David) by provocative settlement programs" and later by unnecessary land confiscations (1981:38). For the settlers of Gush Emunim, the crisis atmosphere begun in September 1978 calmed, as it became clear that the Begin government was still committed to settlement in the West Bank despite the peace treaty and American pressures. But a new crisis for Gush Emunim was brewing. This time it was to be brought by Israel's highest court.

The Crisis Over Land Confiscations

In September 1978, the Supreme Court issued an injunction against all building and development in the settlement of Beit El after twelve Arab landowners from the nearby town of El Bira claimed that their lands had been confiscated illegally for Jewish settlement. Two settlement groups[16] had been preparing to go up to the site, and shortly before the Court order, after being warned of the coming injunction, settlers established Beit El. While development of the site violated the Court's injunction, settlers continued to work to complete construction of the outpost throughout the five-month period that the Court considered the case:

> During this time the army had a unit watching over us so that we wouldn't do any work against the orders of the injunction. Sometimes they looked the other way. Sometimes they went on patrol. Sometimes at night they weren't here. . . . So we did a lot of work on our own.

Although the El Bira–Beit El case was ultimately decided in favor of the settlers, it set the stage for a series of challenges by West Bank Arabs of government confiscation of land for settlement. The most serious of these occurred at Elon Moreh in June, and resulted in a major setback for settlement efforts. In the El Bira–Beit El case, the Supreme Court ruled that the confiscation of land at Beit El was allowable only because of overriding security concerns. Now government promises for the development and expansion of the settlements were slowed as the security justification for other confiscations were challenged. Shortly before the Elon Moreh decision was handed down in October, Gush Emunim settlers staged a large-scale "settle-in" to protest the government's failure to requisition land for the expansion of existing settlements and the development of new ones. The government ordered the security forces to remove the settlers, who had established at least twenty-seven temporary sites.

In the case of Elon Moreh, the Supreme Court argued that political considerations rather than security needs were behind government confiscations of Arab land for the settlement. Thus the Court ruled that the land taken for the development of the site had been illegally seized, and it ordered the dismantling of the settlement within one month (Richardson, 1979).

Prime Minister Begin reacted to the Court decision with a statement that he would find a new site for the settlers as close as possible to the original one. He also promised to establish six new settlements in the West Bank by the end of the year (Wallfish, 1979b). The settlers, who were not satisfied by Begin's initiatives, began preparations to prevent a government move to uproot the site. Gush Emunim activists feared that the dismantling of Elon Moreh would create a precedent for other evacuations from settlements on the West Bank (Brilliant, 1979). Throughout this period, the Begin government worked to avoid a direct confrontation with the Elon Moreh group—going so far as to postpone the date of the evacuation after the settlers refused to move voluntarily. Eventually, the group accepted a nearby site for the settlement, though even after an agreement had been reached a number of settlers would not leave the settlement voluntarily and forced soldiers to carry them away from their homes.

In the year preceding the national elections of June 1981 it became apparent that the government led by Begin and Sharon was interested in an all-out settlement effort in the West Bank. Though limited by the Camp David framework, the government operated at "full steam" and with considerable "aggressiveness" to perpetuate Jewish settlement in the region (Sprinzak, 1981). Large tracts of land were confiscated by Sharon, who had developed a strategy to circumvent the Supreme Court's recent decisions concerning security justifications for land confiscations. Ian Lustick comments:

> Of special importance in this complicated but largely successful effort was the Sharon committee's apprecia-

tion of two loopholes in the High Court's judgment. The first loophole was that the Hague Convention distinguished between privately owned and "public land." While the Court agreed that private individuals whose lands had been seized had legal standing to sue for return of their lands, no representative body exists on the West Bank that can claim standing to sue in Israeli municipal courts for lands seized illegally from the public or "state" domain. . . . Thus only seizures of privately owned land can be prevented or reversed through recourse of the High Court of Justice. . . . The second loophole discovered . . . was that the High Court had refused to intervene in any disputations over the ownership status of a parcel of land. (Lustick, 1981:569–70)

Gush Emunim settlers, fearful of the expected Labor victory in the coming elections, devoted all of their efforts to expanding existing sites and developing the permanent housing that began to sprout in the older settlements. Meanwhile, five new Gush Emunim outposts were established by the government (Chadasha, Carmel, Kochav HaShachar, Michmash, and Yakir).

The "Lessons" of the Sinai Withdrawal

With Begin's surprise election victory in June 1981, the settlers of Gush Emunim breathed a sigh of relief and turned their efforts to preventing a Sinai withdrawal. Though Gush Emunim activists played a major role in protests in Sinai, they did not do so under the auspices of Gush Emunim. Conflicts over tactics, unabashed government support for the settlement enterprise in the West Bank, the emergence of YESHA (The Council of Jewish Settlements in Judea, Samaria and Gaza), Techiyah (a political party representing an alliance between secular and religious advocates of annexation), and the Stop the Withdrawal from Sinai Movement, all helped to bring about the demise of Gush Emunim—the "ideological" movement.[17] The death of Rabbi Kook in early 1982 contributed to this decline as well.

What remained of Gush Emunim was its "settlement organization," Amanah, which had devoted itself primarily to settlement matters and whose leadership, in contrast to that of the Gush Emunim movement itself, was chosen by a governing body comprised of two members from each of the affiliated settlements. What of Gush Emunim's "ideological movement" and its leaders?

> We have a purpose. If it works then it works. If Heaven forbid there was a political situation (in the West Bank) with pressure on settlements like (that) in Sinai—in a week again there will be a big movement. Those involved in politics etc. will return to us. Thank God there is no need for that now.

In Sinai, Amanah settlers were a major source of money and manpower. Besides their settlement at Atzmona, they established another illegal site nearby which was called Chotzer Adar. A settler from Ofra led a group dominated by Amanah settlers in an illegal settlement at the existing site of Talmei Yosef. All told, almost a quarter of the settlers of Amanah spent some time at Sinai settlements showing their solidarity and support against the withdrawal.[18] In March 1981, Amanah settlers were a major force at a protest march that attracted 25,000 antiwithdrawal supporters in Jerusalem (*Jerusalem Post*, 1981).

When the government finally came to uproot the Sinai settlements in March 1982, Amanah settlers in Atzmona, Chotzer Adar, and Talmei Yosef offered passive resistance to soldiers. Though there were scuffles between the settlers and security forces when settlers tried to disrupt the evacuation (e.g., Brilliant, 1982), there were few serious incidents.

For most of the Gush Emunim settlers, Sinai could not be compared directly in importance to the West Bank. Though some argued that it was part of the Land of Israel (at least in its northern parts), the Sinai never held the emotional ties nor the *Halachik* legitimacy of the biblical regions of Judea and Samaria. For Gush Emunim settlers, Sinai was meant as a "lesson" for the rest of Israeli society. The major upheaval that developed in the country and the potential violence of the later weeks of the Sinai protests constituted a warning to other Israelis that the same process would create disastrous consequences if applied to the West Bank. Many Sinai settlers claimed that the government had allowed the antiwithdrawal movement to progress as far as it did for precisely this same purpose (Amrani, 1982a).

Suburbanization and the Norms of Gush Emunim

The Gush Emunim settlements were entering a phase of tremendous growth and development when field research for this study was carried out. In many of the sites, settlers had moved from their sparse caravans to three-and four-bedroom *Villot* (suburban-style housing). The government of Israel had taken as a coalition partner the Techiyah party, and annexation became a reality in deed if not in fact (Shipler, 1982). The settlers were confident that they had "arrived." But still, Sinai had brought home the real possibility of a withdrawal of Israel from the West Bank in exchange for peace. An "impossible nightmare" became a reality in Sinai, and the lesson was not lost on Amanah settlers. Many began to speak seriously of armed resistance to government attempts to uproot West Bank settlement (see chapter 6), and some outside the settlements feared that settlers were stockpiling weapons in preparation for such a crisis (Goell, 1981).

By the summer of 1982, a new generation of settlements were developing in the West Bank (Shafir, 1983). They were built with government pleas to Israelis to "raise their standard of living" and "come live in Samaria." The attraction for settlers became private homes rather than ideology. Large government subsidies were offered to would-be settlers, who could live in suburban-style housing on the West Bank available only to the richest Israelis twenty minutes away on the coastal plain. Yet, for the Gush Emunim settlers there remained one underlying goal behind everything they did. They did not forget that their settlements were founded to prevent the government from carrying out territorial "transgressions":

> And with the idealistic people who live here . . . it will be quite impossible to move Israel from this region. And that's in fact what lies under everything. (Even) if people are talking about the color of curtains in the kitchen . . . they still think about Yamit (a town uprooted during the Israeli withdrawal from Sinai).

3

The Gush Emunim Settlers

The origins of the Gush Emunim movement have been traced to a young national religious generation in Israel which sought to redefine the role religion would play in the Jewish state. At the forefront of this generation stood the future leaders of Gush Emunim, primarily students of Rabbi Zvi Yehuda Kook. In scholarly debate and public discussion, it was to be these Gush Emunim leaders—young men of Ashkenazi ancestry, products of rabbinical academies and Bnai Akiva youth groups and high schools—who dominated images of the social composition and ideological orientations of the movement (e.g., Sprinzak, 1977; Raanan, 1981).

The concern in this chapter is to provide a description of the broader Gush Emunim community that came to dominate the Amanah settlements. I begin with a demographic profile of the Gush Emunim outposts in which characteristics of settlers are compared to those of the general Israeli population. I then develop a typology for distinguishing types of settlers based upon the predominant motivations that sparked Gush Emunim settlement efforts. An examination of the settlers who fall in each of these motivational "clusters,"[1] and their roles in governing the Gush Emunim community, identifies an important link between the success of settlement and the decline of the Gush Emunim movement.

The Gush Emunim Settlers: A Demographic Profile

Compared to the general Israeli Jewish community, the Gush Emunim settlers were a very young group (see Table 3.1). Indeed, more than 90 percent of the settlers surveyed were under forty-five years of age, and over a third were under thirty.[2] Following the general pattern of religious couples in Israel, almost all of the settlers were married, and though young, a third of settler families had four or more children. The settlers were also more likely than other Israelis to have been native-born. Although Gush Emunim is often pictured as a movement especially attractive to new immigrants (e.g., Schnall, 1985; Waxman, 1985), two-thirds of the settlers were born in Israel; of immigrants, fewer than one in five came to the country after 1972.

In terms of their religiosity, settlers show a commitment to Orthodox Judaism evidenced by only a minority of Israel's Jewish citizens. This is reflected, in part, by the degree to

Table 3.1   Demographic Characteristics of Gush Emunim Settlers as Contrasted with the General Israeli Jewish Population

Characteristic[1]	Settlers[2](%)	Israeli Jews[3](%)
Adults under 45 years of age	93	35
Native born	68	53[4]
Orthodox observance	92	20–30
Post-high-school education	66	13[5]
Men with higher *Yeshiva* training	35	3[6]
Ashkenazi ancestry	82	40

[1]All settler characteristics are significantly different ($p < .01$) from those of the general Jewish Israeli population.
[2]Frequencies of settler characteristics in this table (and those that follow) are based on "weighted" or corrected frequencies (see Note 2).
[3]Estimates are drawn from Israel (1982), Weller (1974), and Katz and Gurevitch (1976).
[4]Israelis—Age 20–39.
[5]Israelis—Age 25–35.
[6]Calculated as last school attended in Israel.

which settlers refrained from actions that violate laws of the Jewish Sabbath. Following Orthodox tradition, more than 90 percent of the settlers reported that they did not listen to the radio or watch television on that day. The religious orientations of Gush Emunim settlers are also reflected in the very large number who were educated in Israel's religious public-school system and participated in Bnai Akiva, the national religious youth movement. While the large majority of Israelis attend secular public schools (Rinott, 1972), more than three-quarters of the Gush Emunim settlers educated in Israel (83 percent of the total settler population) attended the religious public-school system. In turn, a majority of the settlers had been involved in Bnai Akiva, a group that accounts for only a small minority of Israel's overall youth-movement membership (see Yadlin, 1972).

On average, Gush Emunim settlers were extremely well educated as compared with other Israelis. Two-thirds of the settlers report having some post-high-school education. A third had college degrees, and of these, almost half acquired some type of secondary university degree. They were also much more likely than Israelis generally to have attended a post-high-school rabbinical academy. More than a third of male settlers report receiving some higher *Yeshiva* training, and of these, almost half studied at Mercaz HaRav, the academy of Rabbi Zvi Yehuda Kook.

In keeping with the image of the "scholar-warrior" fostered by the Gush Emunim movement (Schnall, 1985), few male settlers had utilized deferments provided for those who study at rabbinical academies. Moreover, one in ten male settlers had served their army duty in *Yeshivat Hesder*, a program which allows religious Israelis to combine army duty and *Yeshiva* study, but demands that they spend three extra years in full-time military service. The image of the scholar-warrior was not applied to women in the Gush Emunim movement, and thus they were much more likely to utilize deferments—in this case provided to those who claim that their religious beliefs concerning the role of women in society preclude participation in the military. Only half the settlement women served either in the regular army or in some type of alternative national service.

As was the case with early Gush Emunim activists and leaders, the Gush Emunim settlers trace their ancestry primarily to the Ashkenazi Jewish communities of Europe and the Americas. Some had expected that the movement would bridge the substantial gap between Israel's majority Oriental (Sephardic) Jewish communities, which derive primarily from North Africa and the Middle East, and those from the West. Yet, as Shafir (1985) notes, the movement's religious and traditionalist orientations, in many ways consistent with the general views of the Oriental community in Israel, did not offset the "culture and class gap" between the generally disadvantaged Sephardic Jews and the religious elite identified with Gush Emunim and its settlements.

In sum, the Gush Emunim community in the settlements was drawn from the young national religious generation that spawned the Gush Emunim movement. The settlers were primarily religious Jews of European ancestry, well-educated, who had strong connections with the institutions most closely associated with Gush Emunim. At the same time, there was a degree of diversity in the settlements that was for the most part absent in the cadre of leaders and activists who dominated the early history of the movement.

The Importance of Settlement Motivations

Perhaps more significant than the social origins of Gush Emunim, and indeed the most prominent public feature of the movement in its early years, was the extraordinary dedication of its activists to the cause of settlement in the West Bank. For the leadership of Gush Emunim, settlement lay at the core of the movement's values and ideals. It was seen as the most effective means of preventing government "transgressions" of Jewish territorial norms and ensuring eventual Israeli annexation of the West Bank. Settlement was also a potent symbol of Gush Emunim's links to the idealism of the traditional Zionist enterprise and the importance it placed on pioneering and settlement (Avruch, 1979).

In order to assess the commitment of Gush Emunim settlers to the settlement norms that sparked the Gush Emunim movement, they were presented with a list of possible motives for settling the West Bank[3] and asked what role each of them played in their decision to settle in the region.[4] The choices provided to settlers were drawn from the different motivations identified during in-depth interviews. Some were strongly identified with the Gush Emunim movement. For example, a number of settlers referred to Rabbi Kook's teachings when describing the reasons for their move to the West Bank. Others referred directly to the social control goals of settlement: "Our purpose was to create facts on the Land, to create a Jewish presence in the region . . . [i]n order to prevent the emergence of Arab rule."

A number of settlers voiced more traditional Israeli settlement values when describing their reasons for moving to the region. For them, the norms that underlay Gush Emunim's settlement efforts were generally ignored. Indeed, a number argued that they had little connection with Gush Emunim before moving to the Amanah settlements. Yet, these settlers, like those who identified with Gush Emunim settlement values, saw their actions as primarily altruistic. They often identified the *Mitzvah* (religious commandment) to settle the Land of Israel as the predominant ideal behind their actions, though this motive would apply to settlement in any part of Israel, including regions under Israeli control before 1967.

Perhaps most at odds with the image of Gush Emunim are the quality-of-life considerations that ordinarily dominate our choices of places to settle and raise children. Some settlers spoke of what they described as the safety and insularity of life within the settlements, or the national religious atmosphere that dominated most of these outposts, when explaining their reasons for moving to the West Bank. Others referred to the opportunities for better housing or better schools that could be found in many of the more established settlements. The emergence of these "self-interested" motivations was noted by many in the settlements, though they often argued that such motivations did not interfere with a settler's overall commitment to the settlement enterprise:

> The kind of people we're getting now might be a little less *Daphkanik*. Certainly good people, but the first settlers were the kind of people who said: "Look I'm coming out here and I don't care what kind of living conditions there are. I don't care if I have to quit a very good job to come and live here, and maybe take a poor job. Because I believe very strongly in the idea of settlement." Today, we're getting people who just as strongly believe in the right of Jews to live here. But, they might be saying (as well): "Look, it's a nice place. It has a nice *Chevra* (community of people) and very nice housing." . . . I think that the people we're getting now are looking more at some of the benefits . . .

In Table 3.2 the six major settlement motivations provided in the survey are listed, and the percentage of settlers who identified each as predominant are reported. As is apparent from the table, many settlers listed more than one predominant motivation, and thus some caution must be used in interpreting these simple tabular findings. Nonetheless, it is clear that Gush Emunim settlement values are well-represented among settlers, though only a small minority reported that

Table 3.2   Predominant Settlement Motivations of Gush Emunim Settlers

	(%)	N
Gush Emunim Settlement Motives		
Desire to create a Jewish presence in Judea and Samaria	59	531
Desire to prevent a return of Judea and Samaria to Arab rule	49	531
Teachings of Rabbi Zvi Yehuda Kook	13	531
General Religious Settlement Motives		
Mitzvah to settle the Land of Israel	57	531
Self-Interested Settlement Motives		
Desire to improve quality of life	14	531
Desire to improve environment for children	21	531

the teachings of Rabbi Zvi Yehuda Kook played a predominant role in their settlement decision. The general religious Zionist value—the *Mitzvah* of settlement—is also noted by large numbers of settlers, and a minority larger than that who identify with the teachings of Rabbi Kook reported that self-interested motivations—a desire to improve quality of life or the environment for children—played a predominant role in bringing them to the West Bank.

Settlement Motivation Clusters

A more complex view of the motivations that underlay Gush Emunim settlement is gained by examining the different combinations of motives settlers identified. Using a statistical technique commonly referred to as "cluster analysis,"[5] settlers were placed in five primary groups (or "clusters") which are distinguished by predominant settlement motivations.[6] Importantly, these clusters, and the background characteristics associated with them, provide a unique view of the different types of settlers that make up the Gush Emunim community.

Three of the clusters are linked strongly to Gush Emunim settlement values (Table 3.3), though each group represents a very different image for Gush Emunim settlers. In the largest of these (the "Gush Emunim values" cluster), which includes more than a third of the settlers, the norms of Gush Emunim settlement were predominant, and self-interested motivations played little or no role. Reflecting their settlement motivations, a disproportionate number of these settlers (as compared with the settlement population as a whole) had been active in the Gush Emunim movement (Table 3.4).[7] They were also more likely than any of the other clusters examined to have settled on the West Bank in the earliest years of Gush Emunim's settlement efforts. While this group fits the strongly ideological portrait that is often applied to Gush Emunim activists, the teachings of Rabbi Kook, which were so important to the early leaders of Gush Emunim, are generally ignored (Table 3.3).

Table 3.3 Percentage of Each Settler Cluster Identifying Each Settlement Motivation as Predominant

MOTIVE	Gush Emunim Values	Rabbi Kook Followers	Rounded Concerns	Self-interested	Other Motivations
Create Jewish presence in Judea and Samaria	95%	85%	95%	19%	0%
Prevent return of Judea and Samaria to Arab rule	85	46	92	1	4
Teachings of Rabbi Kook	1	63	23	0	1
Mitzvah to settle the Land of Israel	45	99	95	6	54
Improve quality of life	1	3	55	71	2
Improve environment for children	4	0	91	76	6
N in Sample	179	79	57	62	144
Corrected percent of settlers in each cluster[a]	36	16	10	10	26

[a] See note 2 of chapter 3.

Table 3.4   Selected Settler Characteristics Disproportionately Represented in Each Cluster[a]

Gush Emunim Values
People involved in Gush Emunim before settling (54.7%)[b]
Settlers arriving before 1978 (28.6%)[b]

Rabbi Kook Followers
People involved in Gush Emunim before settling (62.5%)[b]
Higher *Yeshiva* studies (62% of men)[c]
Sabbath observers (96%)[c]

Rounded Concerns
Settlers arriving after 1977 (98.0%)[b]

Self-Interested
People not involved in Gush Emunim before settling (83.6%)[c]
No higher *Yeshiva* studies (94.8%)[b]
Non-Sabbath observers (18.6%)[c]
Settlers arriving after 1980 (47.0%)[b]

Other Motivations
None of the characteristics examined was significantly under- or overrepresented

[a] The characteristics examined were: involvement in Gush Emunim prior to settlement, year of settlement, *Yeshiva* studies, and Sabbath observance. The observed frequencies for each cluster were compared to the overall corrected or "weighted" frequencies for the entire sample.
[b] $P < .01$
[c] $P < .05$

A second cluster, which I term "Rabbi Kook followers," includes fewer than half as many settlers as the first. Yet this cluster provides an image of the Gush Emunim settler closer to that represented by Gush Emunim's activists and leaders. And indeed, these settlers were more likely than any others to have been active in the Gush Emunim movement prior to settlement. Like the "Gush Emunim values" group, few settlers in this cluster identify self-interested factors when describing their settlement motives, and most refer to Gush Emunim settlement norms. But in contrast to the former group, these settlers are also linked strongly to the teachings of Rabbi Zvi Yehuda Kook and show a much greater attachment to the more general religious dimensions of settlement. It is thus not surprising that these settlers are more likely than others to have studied in a rabbinical academy, and even when compared to the general Gush Emunim community, Sabbath observant settlers are overrepresented in this cluster.

The third cluster is similar to the first in its attachments to the norms of Gush Emunim settlement, but is distinguished from both of the groups already examined by the strong concern evidenced for the environment the settlements provided for children and their overall quality of life. This "rounded concerns" cluster, which includes one in ten settlers, is perhaps closest to those described above, who "just as strongly believe in the right of Jews to live" on the West Bank, but who are now looking "at some of the benefits." In keeping with their self-interested settlement motivations, they were unlikely to have come to the settlements during the years of Labor Party rule when these outposts were most rustic.

Two groups of settlers, comprising more than a third of the settlement population, are not strongly linked to settlement values associated with Gush Emunim. In the smaller of the two clusters are settlers who listed concerns with quality of life and environment for children, but who did not refer to any of the "altruistic" motives for moving to the West Bank. This group of "self-interested" settlers is most removed from the strongly ideological image that has dominated views of Gush Emunim activists and leaders. They neither refer to Gush Emunim settlement norms nor the teachings of Rabbi Kook, and they evidence little connection with the general religious Zionist values represented by the *Mitzvah* of settlement. In keeping with their settlement motivations, few settlers in this cluster were active in the Gush Emunim movement, and most came to the settlements after they began to receive expansive government support. Few of these settlers have higher *Yeshiva* training, and as compared with settlers generally, Sabbath observant settlers were underrepresented in this cluster.

The final group may be identified as an "other motivations" cluster since the settlement motives examined here fail to describe the predominant factors that brought these settlers to the West Bank. Though the *Mitzvah* of settlement was listed by a large number of settlers in this group, as noted earlier, this motive could also be applied to settlement within Israel's pre-1967 boundaries, and thus does not tap any special motivation for moving to these controversial territories. We may speculate that these settlers had strong personal (perhaps either emotional or familial) reasons for moving to the West Bank.[8]

Who Rules?

Analysis of settlement motivations shows that a majority of settlers were strongly attached to Gush Emunim settlement values. Yet the cluster that most closely reflects the early activists and leaders of the Gush Emunim movement— "Rabbi Kook Followers"—accounts for only a small minority of the settlement population. An examination of who governs the Gush Emunim community may of course provide a very different view of who predominates in the settlements than does a review of the numerical strength of each of the clusters identified. Just as the students of Rabbi Kook provided the primary leadership of the Gush Emunim movement but attracted a much broader group to its protests and settlement actions, we might expect that the Rabbi Kook followers would exercise a leadership role though they are a small minority in the settlements.

Since the settler clusters are developed from items in the survey, it is difficult to determine directly which of these groups actually played a larger role in governing the settlements. To do so, we would need to identify each leader and place him or her within one of our settler groups. It is possible, on the other hand, to examine the relative participation in leadership positions of settlers in the five clusters identified. In the survey, settlers were asked about fourteen such leadership positions found in most of the Gush Emunim settlements.[9]

As Table 3.5 illustrates, settlers identified with the Gush Emunim values cluster held, on average, almost twice as many leadership positions (per settler) as did any of the other groups. This means, in turn, that these settlers were even more dominant in the absolute number of offices they held, since they were also the most numerous settler type. Rabbi Kook followers, on the other hand, did not play a leadership role greater than that found in the remaining groups. Indeed,

Table 3.5   Average Number of Leadership Positions Held by Settlers in Each of the Five Settler Clusters

Cluster	Mean Number of Positions	Standard Deviation
Gush Emunim values	1.51	2.24
Rabbi Kook Followers	.78	1.25
Rounded concerns	.70	.98
Self-interested	.82	2.00
Other motivations	.83	1.33

Number of cases = 492

in this sample, they held fewer positions, on average, than did the "self-interested" or "other motivations" clusters.

Of the administrative bodies in the settlements, the secretarial and absorption committees played the most crucial roles in the development of these outposts. The secretarial committee was the official governing body in the settlements. It determined both settlement policy and the nature of settlement development. The absorption committee was responsible for screening new members, a responsibility that gave these settlers an important degree of control over the future of these communities. In examining these particular leadership positions, once again the Gush Emunim values cluster is found to play a predominant role in ruling these outposts (Table 3.6). These settlers were considerably more likely than

Table 3.6   Percent Participation in Key Settlement Committees (by cluster)

Cluster	Absorption Committee		Secretarial Committee	
	Member	Chairperson	Member	Chairperson
Gush Emunim values	18.4%	10.1%	23.5%	7.8%
Rabbi Kook Followers	10.1	5.1	16.5	0.0
Rounded concerns	12.3	1.8	12.3	3.5
Self-interested	9.7	3.2	12.9	1.6
Other motivations	10.4	2.1	16.7	1.4

Number of cases = 492

others to have served as members or chairpersons of these committees. At the same time, there was comparatively little variation between the four remaining settler clusters.

In interpreting these findings and their implications for understanding who rules these communities, we must turn to a major difference in governance between the Gush Emunim movement and the settlements it developed. In the Gush Emunim movement generally, leadership was entrusted to a small group, mostly graduates of the Mercaz HaRav *Yeshiva*, whose claim to leadership lay primarily with their charisma and efforts in founding the movement. There was no formal Gush Emunim membership, nor any elections.[10] In contrast, the settlements were governed as small participatory democracies,[11] and those who constituted the largest block of settlers were thus able to assume the predominant leadership role in these communities.

The Success of Settlement and the Decline of the Gush Emunim Movement

The settlers of Gush Emunim were drawn primarily from the young generation of nationalist religious Jews that is strongly associated with the Gush Emunim movement. They were also strongly attached to the values and norms underlying Gush Emunim's settlement efforts. Yet those who made up the rank and file of the Gush Emunim settlements, and indeed its leadership as well, were less attached to the personality and teachings of Rabbi Zvi Yehuda Kook than were Gush Emunim's founders. This fact does not take away from their general commitment to the values underlying Gush Emunim's settlement efforts, but it does shed some light on the decline of the Gush Emunim movement described in the previous chapter.

Neil Smelser (1962) notes that "value oriented"[12] collective movements have a tendency toward disunity or instability. The likelihood that these movements will develop different types of leaders whose objectives differ or come into conflict with one another is one cause of this disunity. Another is the heterogeneity of these movements, a heterogeneity usually not recognized in the early phases of their development. Finally, changes in strategy or tactics are also likely to cause major fissures in the unity of these groups.

While the development of the Gush Emunim settlements represents perhaps Gush Emunim's greatest success, their emergence created two of those conditions Smelser cites for the decline of collective movements. The Sinai experience, as we have already seen, created the third condition (more will be said about this problem in chapter 6). The settlements allowed for the development of new leaders who were less strongly attached to Rabbi Kook and Gush Emunim's founders than to the settlements themselves. They allowed, as well, for the emergence of a body of settlers who represented the broad range of Gush Emunim support. Accordingly, it is not surprising that at precisely that time when the Gush Emunim settlements grew and prospered, the Gush Emunim movement lost its vitality and unity. The development of settlements may be viewed as a major cause of this decline.

4

Vigilantism as Deviant Social Reaction

With Gush Emunim's success in establishing settlements came the reality of dealing with the more than 700,000 Palestinian Arabs who live in the West Bank.[1] For the most part the settlers expected that they would have little to do with Arabs in the region, a position that was encouraged by government settlement agencies (Benvenisti, 1982:47). But the close proximity of Gush Emunim settlements to Arab villages and towns and the scarcity of land for settlement in these areas could not but place the Gush Emunim settlers in direct conflict with their new neighbors. These conflicts, in turn, led them to again use rule-violating actions as a strategy to control behavior they defined as deviant. In this case, though, the target of control was not the Israeli government but West Bank Arabs.

In this chapter the origins of settler efforts to sanction and control Palestinian Arabs is examined. I begin with a review of general settler attitudes toward Arabs in the West Bank.[2] I then turn to a description of settler vigilantism and its role as a strategy of social reaction in the Gush Emunim community. My findings show that settler vigilantism was widely supported in the Gush Emunim settlements. It was also defended and rationalized as a social-control strategy in much the same ways as are legal controls brought as societal reactions. In concluding, the implications of these findings for the detection and prosecution of vigilante violence are examined.

Respect Him and Suspect Him

From the very outset, Arabs in the West Bank have voiced intense opposition to Gush Emunim's settlement efforts (Lesch, 1980; Ma'Oz, 1984),[3] and settlers themselves recognized that they were not welcome in the region. Many settlers admitted that Arabs hated them, and "would be happy" if the settlements disappeared. At the same time, settlers found Arab resentment easy to understand, and a number of those interviewed reported that they would feel similarly if circumstances were reversed: "They would prefer that I would be in Tel Aviv. They see us negatively. . . . The fact that I am here disturbs them. And if I were them, I would think the same."

While settlers thus acknowledged Arab resentment, most believed that the settlements would in the long run be accepted. Settlers often argued that Arabs held no special grudge against settlements in the West Bank, but were opposed to all Jewish settlement in Israel. They did not accept the image of an intense unalterable hatred towards settlers presented by many Middle East observers (e.g., Shipler, 1987; Friedman, 1987a). Indeed, they argued that the majority of Arabs were indifferent to individual settlements and would cooperate with them if Arab fears of the "radical minority" were neutralized. As one settler from Elon Moreh reasoned:

> Basically they don't like us. It is hard to speak of a general attitude. The fear of the Palestine Liberation Organization dominates here. They must identify with the radicals. They make the point, and everybody else follows it. I think that if they were convinced that we are here to stay, the majority would accept us.

Most settlers felt that Arabs who accept Israeli rule and the existence of Jewish settlements have a "right" to live on the West Bank. At the same time, many argued that settlers must be careful not to "encourage" Arabs to remain in the region. Thus, while traditional Zionist ideologies called for the employment of only Jewish labor as a way to avoid the exploitation of non-Jews, a similar rule in the Amanah settlement movement took on a very different meaning for many settlers. As a Gush Emunim representative in Jerusalem explained:

> The organization (Amanah) does not say to take the Arabs and expel them. But in my view we don't need to encourage them to be here by giving them work. . . . If I give them work, I am giving them a reason for remaining (in this region). . . . ([B]y refusing to give them work) I am not doing something active (to encourage them to leave), but I am doing something passive.

Ironically, almost all of the settlements were built by West Bank Arab workers employed by Israeli construction firms.

A minority of settlers characterized relations between the settlements and local Arab villages and towns as "good" (Table 4.1), though many claimed to be interested in developing

Table 4.1   Settler/Arab Relations

STATEMENT: "This settlement has good relations with Arabs in the area."

Response	(%)
Strongly disagree	10.2
Disagree	36.2
No opinion	22.6
Agree	26.4
Strongly agree	4.6

Number of cases = 481

Table 4.2   Developing Contacts with Arabs

STATEMENT: "Settlers should try to develop contacts with Arabs."

Response	(%)
Strongly disagree	11.7
Disagree	24.6
No opinion	17.9
Agree	34.4
Strongly agree	11.4

Number of Cases = 507

future contacts with Arabs in these areas (Table 4.2). Whether speaking of present or future relations, few settlers voiced a desire to develop strong social or friendship ties. As one settler remarked:

> We must come to a general understanding with the Arabs . . . we have to develop more bonds with them if we want to live here. So in the end we must have neighborly relations. (But) I don't believe that we will have social contacts. They will have to see us in a positive light because we provide them with economic opportunities.

A few settlers described visits to a villager's house for tea or invitations offered villagers to homes at the settlements. But for most, "good relations" included buying vegetables in a nearby village or contracting with West Bank Arabs for temporary labor.

For settlers, the overall picture of their relationship with Arabs in this region is captured in a phrase they repeated quite often—*Kabdehu Va Chashdehu*—"respect him and suspect him." Jewish settlers claimed that they wanted peaceful relations with neighboring Arab villages and towns, but they kept their distance and were distrustful:

> There has to be a vigilant attitude, but that doesn't mean we should hate anyone. *Kabdehu Va Chashdehu.* We have to be extremely careful. We cannot be weak (when dealing with the Arabs), but rather we must be strong and forceful.

This strength, in turn, was generally translated by settlers into a willingness to take the law into their own hands when they believed that their lives or interests were threatened.

Settler Vigilantism

Vigilantism is a form of establishment violence. It involves "acts or threats of coercion in violation of the formal boundaries of an established socio-political order which, however, are intended by the violators to defend that order from some form of subversion" (Rosenbaum and Sederberg, 1976:4). Vigilantism is in essence citizens "taking the law into their own hands" (Brown, 1975:95–96; Little and Sheffield, 1983:797), though it often involves efforts to subdue and control disadvantaged or pariah social groups (Sederberg, 1978). For the most part Gush Emunim vigilantism was intended as a response to Arab law-breaking—primarily stoning attacks on settler vehicles.[4] But as will be described later, vigilante actions by settlers were also intended to play a broader role in establishing Jewish dominance in these territories.

Settlers described their involvement in a variety of vigilante actions, and claimed that their form was dependent upon the type of Arab "harassments" they sought to control. As one settlement leader from a particularly troublesome area north of Ramallah explained:

> Our attitude has been that we cannot afford to allow any action of hostility by the Arabs to go unanswered. . . . If during the day or night a rock was thrown by x amount of Arabs (at a car) . . . we will go out and react. Now what "reaction" means really depends on the situation. We sometimes go talk to the Muktar (the village head) and warn him. Sometimes we try to catch the kids or the people whoever it is who was responsible for what was done. The general idea as I have said, is that we have found that if we don't react, the Arabs will translate this as a sign of weakness. And once we're in that situation, we really don't have any point of strength to make sure this wouldn't happen again.

Most often settler vigilantism involved the destruction of property. Settlers would, for example, effectively shut down a school or business by welding its locks, or drive through a town breaking the windows of cars. Sometimes they would rely upon less serious actions, such as roadblocks, to "punish" Arabs in the region. For the most part, settlers used collective punishments, focusing upon the village or town where trouble began rather than the specific individuals involved. One settlement leader, who described his community as more moderate than most of the settlements in his area, gave two examples of such vigilante actions:

> There was one time when we took an action after . . . our bus with kindergarten kids was bombarded (by stones). . . . The next morning from six to seven-thirty, around the area where the incident happened, we made a blockade in both directions, not letting any traffic . . . go by. . . . I can't say for sure whether that had a good lasting effect on the Arabs. Maybe it had an effect in the sense that they knew that if they overstepped their bounds we're here and would take the law into our own hands, because the Army would not do enough. . . .
>
> There was one other incident. . . . There was a period of a couple of weeks where almost every day there were incidents . . . and nothing helped. . . . We had a meeting . . . and we went out in a couple of cars. . . . The Arabs claimed 150 windows were broken on that night. . . . We threw a lot of stones, we didn't count. . . . Nobody was hurt during that action and it of course brought a lot of rain on our heads from the military government, but no one was fingered.

Actual or threatened physical violence was also used as a control strategy by settlers. They often beat or threatened Arab youths they suspected of throwing stones. In some cases they seized Arabs and brought them to the settlements for "interrogation." A leader in an older Gush Emunim settlement described their use of threats in dealing with a village leader (Muktar) from an area where cars were being stoned:

> We sent representatives to the Muktar of the village. And we said that for the good of everyone concerned they should not throw stones in the future. And if we catch someone that throws a stone, we will break all his bones.

Settler vigilantism was a community-supported strategy of control in which a large number of settlers participated. More than three-quarters of survey respondents supported the general principle of settlers acting independently of government authority in response to "Arab harassments" (Table 4.3).[5] This

Table 4.3   Settler Support for Vigilantism

STATEMENT: "It is necessary for settlers to respond quickly and independently to Arab harassments of settlers and settlements."

Response	(%)
Strongly disagree	1.6
Disagree	13.2
No opinion	9.1
Agree	28.5
Strongly agree	47.6

Number of Cases = 404

Table 4.4   Percentage Support for Vigilantism (by settlement)

Settlement	Strongly Disagree	Disagree	No Opinion	Agree	Strongly Agree	N
Atzmona	0%	0%	0%	47%	53%	15
Beit Choron	14	24	10	19	33	21
Beit El	0	6	19	31	44	16
Beit El Bet	0	9	18	23	50	22
Beit Yatir	0	4	0	41	55	22
Carmel	0	17	0	33	50	12
Chadasha	0	8	15	39	39	13
Elon Moreh	0	4	8	36	52	25
Kaddumim	0	19	6	38	38	16
Karnei Shomron	0	29	0	18	53	17
Kfar Adumim	11	18	7	32	32	28
Kfar Tapuach	0	22	0	33	44	18
Kochav HaShachar	0	22	7	41	30	27
Mevoh Dotan	0	12	0	19	69	16
Michmash	0	15	8	31	46	13
Mispe Yerecho	0	22	22	56	0	9
Neve Tzuf	4	4	4	37	52	27
Ofra	0	7	21	7	64	14
Sheve Shomron	0	11	22	17	50	18
Shilo	6	0	0	31	63	16
Tekoah	0	0	7	29	64	14
Yakir	5	20	10	20	45	20

Table 4.5   Percentage of Reported Settler Participation in Vigilante
Behavior (by sex)[a]

Type	Male	Female
No participation stated	68.6%	94.3%
Roadblocks	3.0	1.0
Meeting (threats of future "sanctions")	4.8	0.8
Destruction of property	3.7	0.9
Detention or dispersal of persons	2.5	1.2
Threat of physical violence	2.5	0.0
Physical violence, firing of weapons[b]	2.8	0.4
Other vigilante actions[c]	12.1	1.4

Number of cases = Male, 208; Female, 268

[a]Only the most serious action reported by settlers is included.
[b]Incidents where settlers fired their weapons while the subject of an Arab attack are
not included as vigilante actions. Settlers are required by military order to travel
armed in the West Bank, and they are empowered to use their weapons when lives are
threatened. Thus, settlers perceive the use of weapons in direct response to Arab
"harassments" as a form of legal, as opposed to vigilante, control.
[c]In a large number of these cases, settlers noted vigilante behavior but did not specify
its type.

Table 4.6   Reported Participation of Male Settlers in Vigilantism (by
settlement)

Settlement	No Participation	Participation	Not Stated	N
Atzmona	1	6	2	9
Beit Choron	8	5	0	13
Beit El	2	4	3	9
Beit El Bet	10	1	1	12
Beit Yatir	2	7	0	9
Carmel	2	4	1	7
Chadasha	4	2	0	6
Elon Moreh	2	11	2	15
Kaddumim	12	1	0	13
Karnei Shomron	11	1	1	13
Kfar Adumim	13	2	0	15
Kfar Tapuach	4	3	3	10
Kochav HaShachar	8	6	0	14
Mevoh Dotan	7	1	0	8
Michmash	7	3	2	12
Mispe Yerecho	8	2	1	11
Neve Tzuf	5	4	1	10
Ofra	6	6	0	12
Sheve Shomron	6	0	0	6
Shilo	1	4	5	10
Tekoah	5	1	2	8
Yakir	9	1	0	10

support for vigilantism was found in each of the twenty-two settlements examined.[6] In every outpost a majority of settlers surveyed supported vigilante actions (Table 4.4).

Almost a third of the male settlers admitted involvement in some type of vigilante behavior, though few women reported participation in vigilantism (Table 4.5).[7] While the extent of reported participation varied widely across the settlements (Table 4.6), in all but one outpost studied there was some admitted involvement in criminal responses to Arab "harassments." Of the male settlers who identified the type of vigilante action they carried out, one in seven claimed to have used physical violence or fired weapons with serious intent, and one in five claimed to have destroyed Arab property.[8]

Defending and Rationalizing Deviant Social Reaction

Similarities between legal and vigilante control have generally been found in the goals that underlie these forms of social action (e.g., Brown, 1976; Stone, 1979; Little and Sheffield, 1983). Both legal justice and vigilantism seek to control crime or disorder. In many settings they have even been seen as playing complementary roles in a wider "justice" system (Brown, 1971). Examination of settler vigilantism suggests that the resemblance between vigilante and legal control extends much further. In the following pages I detail a striking similarity between settler rationalizations for the vigilante phenomenon and those that underlie societal reactions to deviance. These are reflected in explanations for the emergence of vigilantism, defenses of its legitimacy, and discussion of its effectiveness and costs as a social-control strategy.

The "Failure" of Legal Control

In explaining the development of legal forms of social control, a number of scholars have made reference to the failures of alternative control systems. Schwartz (1954) found, for example, that legal institutions were more likely to develop in communities where face-to-face interactions and other types of informal social controls were ineffective. In a more general statement of this proposition, Black argues that law varies with "every other kind of social control" (1976:109), and that the "quantity of law increases as the quantity of social control" of other types decreases (Black, 1976:65).

In explaining the development of vigilantism, settlers also referred to the absence of alternative social controls, though in this case legal rather than informal control was seen to be ineffective. Settlers argued that it was necessary for them to take the law into their own hands because the military government in Judea and Samaria failed to provide sufficient protection from Arab law-breaking. Most often they supported their claims with reference to the stoning of settler vehicles, though inadequate government responses to threats made to individual settlers, shootings, and stabbings were also cited as causes of vigilante violence.[9]

Stoning incidents usually involved teenagers or younger children throwing rocks (often large enough to break a windshield) at settler cars. Almost half of the settlers reported that they had been victims of such attacks, and over a quarter claimed to have been victimized on more than one occasion (Table 4.7). In ten settlements more than 60 percent of the settlers reported being attacked at least once, and in five settlements these incidents were so common that more than seven in every ten settlers were victimized (Table 4.8).

Rocks thrown at vehicles might be seen as a harmless teenage prank. But such actions are punishable by prison terms in

Table 4.7   Percentage of Settlers Victimized in Stoning Incidents

Incidence	(%)
None	50.4
Once	23.0
More than once	26.6

Number of cases = 508

Table 4.8   Percentage of Settlers Victimized in Stoning
Incidents (by settlement)

Settlement	Never	Once or More	N
Atzmona	23%	77%	17
Beit Choron	46	54	26
Beit El	32	68	22
Beit El Bet	33	67	27
Beit Yatir	43	57	23
Carmel	36	64	14
Chadasha	67	33	12
Elon Moreh	29	71	24
Kaddumim	66	34	29
Karnei Shomron	86	14	29
Kfar Adumim	71	29	28
Kfar Tapuach	33	67	18
Kochav HaShachar	21	79	28
Mevoh Dotan	68	32	19
Michmash	42	58	24
Mispe Yerecho	75	25	24
Neve Tzuf	38	62	29
Ofra	21	79	29
Sheve Shomron	83	17	24
Shilo	19	81	21
Tekoah	75	25	16
Yakir	84	16	25

Israel and were viewed by settlers as threatening and dangerous (Reich, 1984; Friedman, 1987a). Stoning incidents influenced settler decisions on where and when to travel. Hus-
bands often expressed particular concern with the dangers
that their wives or children faced during routine shopping
trips or daily commutation to schools. While there have been
serious injuries and even fatalities as a result of stonings in the
West Bank, only one settler of 539 surveyed claimed to have
received injuries requiring hospitalization from stoning incidents (though sixteen reported being hurt as a result of these
attacks). Whatever the actual risk posed by such incidents, in
the minds of settlers they represented a serious potential
threat to their safety and were a constant reminder of the
"absence" of effective legal control in the region.

Settlers argued that effective social control of Arab law-breaking must include responses to all incidents whether they involved legally serious matters or not. As one settlement leader who advocated this policy explained:

> We are not willing to let the situation get like that here (i.e., daily stoning incidents). Every day we have a car driving through village A and village B, and we react to everything, no matter how small. That is to say, if they throw a stone or something like that, we are not running away, but rather we get out (of the car) and catch the boy and "hit" him—in order that the situation won't deteriorate. Once you don't react to that, the next day there will be three stones, not just one.

Settlers argued that the government did not fulfill its obligation to respond forcefully to Arab harassments of settlers. They attributed this "inaction" partially to legal constraints and government fears of international reactions to more serious social control measures directed at Arabs. Yet this "failure" of governmental control is due in great part to the definitions of deviance held by settlers.

In their view the military authorities did not take Arab "harassments" seriously enough. This is well-illustrated in a comparatively minor incident that occurred near a settlement that claimed to have generally good relations with nearby villagers. Students from a local school had set up stone roadblocks near the outpost that made it difficult for settlers, many of whom commuted to work every day, to leave the area. On the first day of the action, settlers contacted the military government, but no action was taken. After the second day the local military authorities called the settlement and warned them not to take matters into their own hands (in anticipation of a settlement reaction). Finally, "leaders" in the settlement met to discuss the matter, and agreed to vandalize a local Arab school.[10] For settlers, the military authorities had inaccurately defined Arab deviance and "forced" them to take the law into their own hands.

A number of settlement leaders spoke of an "Arab mentality" when explaining the necessity for settler vigilantism. They argued that the government could not deal effectively with Arab law-breaking even if it wanted to. According to this view, it was absolutely essential that settlers respond independently. As one settlement leader reasoned:

> There have to be good relations with the Arabs, as far as possible. But, one has to show firmness if they make trouble. Because the mentality of the Arabs is such that they are used to the situation that people with power have to show their power. If someone throws a stone at you, you don't walk over and say *Shalom* (peace) etc. . . . Rather, first of all, you throw two stones at him, and afterwards *Sulchah* (meeting of reconciliation).

The failures of governmental social control were thus independent of the "quantity of control" exercised by the military. In this settler view, regardless of how seriously the government sanctioned Arab residents, there would be a failure of legal control in the West Bank.

Settler explanations for the emergence of vigilantism were very similar to those that underlie legal control. Yet our findings provide a slightly different picture of the relationship between alternative control systems than that evidenced in other studies (Schwartz, 1954; Black, 1976; for the case of vigilantism, see Little and Sheffield, 1983). Settler views of the effectiveness of legal responses to Arab law-breaking were strongly influenced by their understanding of "Arab deviance" and their disagreements with legal authorities over definitions of the seriousness of Arab "harassments." For settlers there was a subjective perceptual element that shaped the community's beliefs concerning the ineffectiveness of governmental social control. Settler vigilantism varied directly with these settler perceptions, rather than with the objective quantity of control that was exercised by the Israeli government.

The Legitimacy of Vigilante Controls

The legitimacy of a control strategy plays an important part in its emergence in legal control systems (e.g., Friedman, 1977). Though defending criminal social control, settlers were also concerned with the legitimacy of their actions. They found support for assuming the vigilante role in reference to their responsibilities as agents of legal control in the West Bank. They defended their use of collective punishments in reference to control strategies employed by the Israeli government against Arabs in the region.

Settlers were issued automatic weapons for self-defense during travel on the West Bank and were encouraged to see themselves as part of a wider net of Israeli social control in these areas. In this regard, more than one in six male settlers (and one in sixteen women) reported using their weapons in direct response to "Arab harassments" (Table 4.9). These incidents, often more serious than vigilante actions, were seldom defined by the Israeli military authorities as criminal behavior, and as a result the government initiated few investigations of settlers.[11] In turn, settlers did not see any substantial difference between these "legal" actions and settler vigilantism.

Some settlers defended vigilante actions as legitimate precisely because they were less likely to result in serious injuries than immediate "legal" responses to Arab stone-throwing. One settlement leader gave the example of instructions (later rescinded) given by a representative of the military government as to general policy concerning use of weapons. The official told the settlers to begin by shooting above the heads of youths who were throwing stones. But he also assured them that they were allowed to shoot directly at the youths if stone-throwing continued, regardless of whether settlers could safely avoid firing their weapons. The settler interviewed argued that he had no moral problems with settler vigilantism carried out by his outpost, though he felt morally uncomfortable with these "legal" responses to Arab harassments.

Table 4.9   Percentage of Settlers Firing Weapons in Response to "Arab Harassments" (by sex)

Response	Male	Female
Weapon not fired	83.5%	93.6%
Weapon fired	16.5	6.4

Number of cases = Male, 194; Female, 254

Many settlers served their army-reserve duty with regional patrols on the West Bank.[12] As the army is responsible for controlling disorder in the region, settlers responded in army uniform to many of the same forms of Arab law-breaking that were linked to settler vigilantism. Settlers as soldiers also played a more routine role in policing Arabs in these areas. As part of the army's efforts to ensure security and prevent terrorism, they were responsible for checking Arab identity cards or vehicles at army checkpoints. When settlers served reserve duty in the West Bank they thus acted as agents of legal authority in their dealings with their Arab neighbors. Again, the transition to vigilante actions did not represent a major role change for settlers.

The Zionist belief in self-reliance also played an important part in legitimizing settler vigilantism, much as the revolutionary belief in self-reliance played a role in legitimating vigilante committees on the Western frontier (Little and Sheffield, 1983). Settlers felt that they were primarily responsible for the fate of settlement in Judea and Samaria. They began the settlement enterprise with little government support and much opposition. Their success in settling against the government's wishes had, in turn, given them confidence in taking matters into their own hands. They had been self-reliant and believed this to be a general quality of Zionist renewal in Israel. Passivity was seen by them as a sign of the *Gola* ("Jewish exile"). This is well-illustrated by one settlement leader in his description of an incident involving Arabs from a nearby village:

> Once one of our guys went out with sheep and was attacked with knives. . . . We knew (the attacker); he was from Arab village A, and we came there—eight men with guns—and we surrounded the house and all the village came out. And this guy was in the house like a poisoned mouse—he was sure we were going to kill him.
>
> (Did the Arabs call the Military Government?)
>
> No, nothing. They saw that they had business with someone who is not a typical Jew and didn't act like Jews usually act on such an occasion. . . . Usually what

Jews do is what we were taught to do in the *Gola* . . . to say it's okay, next time we'll be good boys or to go crying to the police . . . which is too stupid and inefficient to solve such problems. . . .

Settlers found support for the legitimacy of collective punishments in the responses of legal authorities to Arabs in the West Bank. The Israeli military has from the beginning of the Israeli occupation relied upon collective punishments as a means of controlling Arab violence in the region. For the most part, this strategy of control included closing shops or establishing curfews over villages or towns after disturbances or terrorist incidents. In some cases the government would destroy the house of a "terrorist's" family, leaving the ruins as a lesson to others. Following the lead of their government, settlers claimed that collective punishments are directed at those who are ultimately "responsible" for stoning attacks or other harassments. In the eyes of settlers, Arab youths would not be throwing stones if they did not have at least passive support from adults in their communities.

The Effectiveness of Vigilante Controls

The rationality of social control is determined in reference to the balance between its effectiveness and costs (Parsons, 1951). The effectiveness of legal control is generally measured in terms of the success of the control strategy in preventing future law violations (e.g., Chambliss, 1967). Nevertheless, there are other goals of legal social control. Among them are a desire to uphold the normative values of the community (e.g., Erikson, 1966; Andenaes, 1971; in the case of vigilantism, see Stone, 1979), or to show the general strength and dominance of a particular social group (e.g., Diamond, 1971; also see Rosenbaum and Sederberg's discussion of "social-group-control" vigilantism, 1974). Settlers believed that vigilantism was both an effective deterrent to Arab law-breaking and a means for expressing the eventuality of Jewish control in these areas. In turn, they argued that vigilante actions had few real costs for the Gush Emunim community.

In almost every incident described by settlers, they claimed that problems with Arabs cleared up after their vigilante actions. Indeed, some settlers spoke of vigilantism as if it were a "quick treatment" for dealing effectively with Arab "harassments." This may be compared to military reactions to Arabs in the region, which were often described as having little or no effect upon Arab behavior.[13] Description of an action against a local Arab school provides a typical example of settler confidence in the effectiveness of vigilante controls:

> There is a high school down the road and there were a few incidents where they threw stones at peoples' cars. And the men went out and they took welding instruments, and they welded the metal frameworks on the windows and the doors. And that school was closed for something like three months. Since then nobody has thrown any stones.

While settlers believed that vigilantism was an extremely effective strategy in controlling Arabs in local villages and towns,[14] they did not recognize that their actions may have led to greater resentment on the part of Arabs in the region. Rather, settlers argued that most Arab villagers and city dwellers respect power and, indeed, expect it to be shown. In their view, their vigilante activities played a major role in keeping Arab violence under control and did not contribute greatly to tensions between Jews and Arabs in the West Bank.

We may as well attribute settler support for the effectiveness of vigilantism to their view that they represent the future rulers of these areas. Most settlers believed that Judea and Samaria would be annexed "within the next five years" (Table 4.10), though only a small minority supported granting West Bank Arabs the right to become Israeli citizens or vote in Israeli elections (Table 4.11). Whatever the actual effectiveness of vigilantism in deterring Arab law-breaking, settlers argued that their actions were important if the Arabs were to believe that they intended to remain in the West Bank and determine its future. Jewish settler crime was thus a form of "social-group-control" vigilantism (Rosenbaum and

Table 4.10   Settler Attitudes Toward Annexation of the West Bank

STATEMENT: "Israeli law will be applied to all of Judea and Samaria within the next five years."

Response	(%)
Strongly disagree	3.3
Disagree	6.2
No opinion	19.8
Agree	25.5
Strongly agree	45.2

Number of cases = 478

Table 4.11   Settler Support for Arab Citizenship and Voting

STATEMENT: "If Judea and Samaria are officially annexed, local Arabs should be granted Israeli citizenship and given the right to vote."

Response	(%)
Strongly disagree	37.7
Disagree	33.4
No opinion	14.4
Agree	12.3
Strongly agree	2.2

Number of cases = 481

Sederberg, 1976; see also Lebow, 1976; Potholm, 1976). It provided a means for settlers to show the power of the Jewish settlement movement in the West Bank.

The Costs of Settler Vigilantism

In legal control, it is generally the demands made upon fiscal budgets, possible political fallout, or the dangers that agents of control face in enforcement policies that are weighed against a strategy's overall benefits. Yet for the Gush Emunim settlers, it was primarily legal sanctions or political pressures that provided the most serious potential costs to their communities.

In fact, few settlers were arrested for vigilante acts and none interviewed in this study received any significant sanctions for their behavior. This is not to say that there were not prosecutions for vigilante actions, but rather that Arab complaints about vigilantism were seldom followed up to the point of prosecution (see also Karp, 1983). Even where the military had begun to take action against settlers, government pressure often subsided after a short period. Thus, for example, at one settlement the military tried to take away the weapons of settlers after a well-publicized vigilante incident. The settlers refused to give up their weapons, and as one settler remarked: "There were afterwards discussions and we closed the issue."

Settlers believed that local military commanders were for the most part sympathetic and even supportive of their vigilante acts provided they were kept within certain bounds. As a settlement leader from one of the older settlements argued: "The army encourages us and supports us, and is definitely on our side, but there is a limit. Formally they cannot agree to do everything which we think is necessary to do."

The actual degree of military government support for vigilantism before and during the period of study is difficult to assess because of the obvious reluctance of settlers to discuss these matters. It should be kept in mind that there was often only one or a small number of settlements in the areas directly involved in a vigilante incident, and thus it was not difficult to discover the source of these activities. In the case of one vigilante action, for example, a settlement leader noted that they were questioned after a vigilante incident since the settlement was the only Jewish outpost in the area. Their response was that "we didn't do it," and according to settlers this ended the matter for the authorities.

A few settlers pointed toward the direct assent of the military authorities to vigilante acts. In one particularly striking example of this problem, a settler described the visit of a local commander to the settlement after an Arab complaint that the settlers had destroyed public property in their village:

> They (the military government) came to check who did it, and they couldn't prove who did it. . . . (They) said that that was a good idea (i.e., the vigilante act). . . . They just suggested that next time we do private homes

and not public buildings, because the government has to pay for damage to public property. . . . We have a lot of support from the military government, quite a lot of support.

There was some confusion among settlers about the political costs of their behavior. On the one hand, many argued that they did not want their vigilante activities to get too much publicity because it could reflect badly upon the settlement movement. Yet other settlers felt that the public would sympathize with settler vigilantism and view them as performing an important function were their activities more broadly known. They were also concerned that such a situation might lead to tighter controls over their behavior, which they viewed as a dangerous move in terms of their own security. In fact, the disclosures of an Israeli Attorney General's report on Jewish settler violence against Arabs on the West Bank (Karp, 1983) led to a government crackdown on vigilante behavior in the region (e.g., Shipler, 1984a). In this sense, vigilantism by Jewish settlers may be seen as a type of institutionalized deviance (Williams, 1962), tolerated by the local control system only as long as it did not attract the attentions of the larger society.

Controlling Vigilantism: Problems of Intelligence and Definition

While settlers focused upon the relative lack of legal control brought against vigilante actions, there is evidence that legal authorities were often frustrated in their attempts to investigate and prosecute vigilante violence. In part this resulted from the collective character of vigilantism in the settlements. Vigilantes carried out a strategy of control that was broadly discussed and supported in these outposts. As documented above, these were social reactions, not isolated criminal acts by fringe elements in the settlements. Accordingly, when legal authorities did try to investigate settler crimes, they found that settlement communities shielded vigilantes from prosecution (see also Shipler, 1984b). Even in the case of capital crimes, settlers often refused to cooperate with the authorities (e.g., *Davar*, 1983).[15]

Difficulties in mobilizing societal reactions against settlers also developed from the similarities between vigilante and legal controls. Settlers rationalized and explained their criminality in reference to concepts of legitimacy and effectiveness. They claimed that they worked in support of the established order and acted only because of the failures of legal control in the region. Accordingly, while settler behavior violated the formal boundaries of legality, it was difficult for the wider society to define their acts as crimes.

The case of the "Jewish Underground" provides a troubling example of this confusion. More than twenty Jews, many of them drawn from the leadership of West Bank settlements (Friedman, 1985a), were arrested for a series of violent attacks against Arabs in the region.[16] These included an armed attack on the Islamic University in Hebron in which three people were killed and thirty-three wounded, an attempted bombing of Arab-owned civilian buses, and the maiming of two West Bank Arab mayors by car bombs. While a number of settlers appeared aghast at the extent of the violence involved (Shipler, 1984c), those who carried out these actions defended them in much the same way as the settler vigilantism we have examined (Reich, 1984). They argued that the government had failed to respond to murders of Jewish civilians by West Bank Arabs. They believed that there was a "security vacuum" in the West Bank that forced the settlers to take up arms (Friedman, 1985a). They saw their violence as collective punishments directed at the wider Arab community responsible for West Bank disorders.

Support for those indicted came not only from Israeli settlers but from a substantial minority of the Israeli population (HaAretz, 1984). In the Israeli press, the view that settlers had taken the "law" into their own hands gained "wide currency" (Shipler, 1987:131). The ambivalence these actions provoked among legal control agents was reflected in the treatment of the suspects. Though arrested for capital crimes, they were given a number of privileges unheard of in serious criminal cases. Indeed, they were at one point even taken for a swimming outing by police officers on their return from court—a fact that emerged only because one of the suspects almost drowned (*New York Times*, 1985). The atmosphere in the court itself was "more like a picnic than a judicial proceeding":

> At one of the preliminary hearings, the accused, all in Yarmulkes and full beards, sat among their relatives in the cramped courtroom on Arab East Jerusalem's Saladin Street. They chatted casually with their wives and friends, came and went at will from the courtroom, smiled frequently—though in a somewhat forced way, I thought—prayed, meditated, exchanged food and letters, and otherwise had a fine time. During recesses their police guards allowed them to mingle with their families in the hallway practically unsupervised, a leniency unimaginable in cases involving Arab terrorists. A policeman even stopped a defendant in the corridor and shook his hand warmly. (Shipler, 1987:132–33)

While fifteen settlers were eventually convicted, with three receiving life sentences (mandatory in murder convictions), the court sanctions were generally lenient considering the seriousness of the crimes involved. As one defense lawyer noted: "The sentence gave expression to the special situation to which what is called the 'underground' operated" (Friedman, 1985b). Following the court decision, a number of Israeli politicians, including Foreign Minister Yitzchak Shamir, who referred to the prisoners as "basically good boys" gone astray, claimed that they would fight for amnesty for those sentenced. More generally, the trial had illustrated the confusion that accompanies prosecution of deviance that is developed and rationalized in ways similar to legal social control.

5

Explaining Vigilantism

Chapter 4 focused upon the general attitudes and values that underlay settler violence against West Bank Arabs. Overall, my findings led to the conclusion that settler vigilantism was widely supported and defended as a strategy of deviant social reaction. Yet the data also pointed to a significant degree of variation in both support for and participation in vigilante behavior within the Gush Emunim settlements. For example, only a minority of settlers admitted that they took part in vigilante actions (see Table 4.5) and one in seven reported opposition to vigilantism as a control strategy (Table 4.3). The concern in this chapter will be to identify the characteristics of settlers and the communities in which they lived that help explain this variation in vigilante attitudes and behavior.

My approach to this problem is somewhat different than that taken by other scholars. Studies of vigilantism have relied primarily upon qualitative research methodologies, seldom going beyond a simple listing of vigilante movements or events (e.g., Brown, 1975). Examination of vigilante activists themselves has been even more limited, with impressionistic observations providing for the bulk of scholarly discussion (e.g., Kreml, 1976; Sederberg, 1978). In contrast, my data allow a systematic quantitative review of both individual attitudes toward and participation in vigilantism. They provide, in turn, strong empirical evidence for understanding vigilantism as a form of deviant social reaction.

Explaining Vigilante Attitudes

In trying to explain why some settlers were more or less supportive of vigilantism,[1] or indeed why some were even strongly opposed, a series of explanatory variables are examined in the context of one multivariate regression analysis.[2] This allows an assessment of the relative importance of different factors in explaining vigilantism, while controlling for the confounding influences that one factor may have upon another.

In selecting variables to include in this analysis, I rely primarily upon the discussion of vigilante behavior in chapter 4. But other potential influences on settler attitudes that are suggested by other studies or the special Israeli context of this study are also taken into account. All of the variables included in the analysis are listed in Table 5.1.

Rationalizations of Vigilante Actions

Settlers defended vigilantism in reference to the failures of governmental social control. Thus we would expect those settlers who had personally experienced this "failure"—like victims of stoning incidents—to evidence stronger support for vigilante behavior. In fact, "individual victimization" has a statistically significant effect upon vigilante attitudes (Table 5.2). Those who report being stoned by Arabs show much stronger support for vigilantism than do other settlers.

Given this finding, it is surprising that the overall level of victimization in a settlement has an influence on vigilante attitudes (of about the same magnitude as individual victimization) in precisely the opposite direction. After taking into account their own experiences, those settlers who lived in outposts where a large number of their neighbors had been the subject of stoning attacks were less supportive of vigilante violence. This seems to imply, in contrast to what settlers argued in qualitative interviews, that a failure of legal control near a settlement leads to less sympathy for vigilante actions. Yet the discussion of vigilantism in chapter 4 suggests that this measure may reflect a different dimension in settler rationalizations of vigilante behavior.

Table 5.1   Variables Examined in Analysis of Vigilante Attitudes

Variable	Measurement
Deviant Social Reaction Model	
Rationalizations for Vigilantism	
Individual victimization	Binary, other settlers versus those who state they have been victimized in a stoning incident
Settlement victimization	Interval scale[a]; range = .15–1.47
Army base	Binary; settlements not located at an army base versus others
Arab vote	Binary; other settlers versus those who support granting Arabs voting rights in the case of annexation
Social distance	Five-category ordinal scale; range = "strongly disagree" to "strongly agree"[b]
Messianism	Five-category ordinal scale; range = "strongly disagree" to "strongly agree"[c]
Socialization to Vigilante Norms	
Group attitudes	Interval scale; range = 3.18–4.60[d]
Settlement size	Interval scale; range = 16–132
Leadership	Binary; other settlers versus those who served as "Settlement Secretary" or "Chair of Secretarial Committee"
Year of settlement	Interval scale; range = 69–82[e]
Other Variables	
Settlement motivation	Five categorical variables
Religiosity	Binary; Sabbath-observant settlers versus others;
Ethnicity	Binary; Western versus North African/Middle Eastern Origins
Education	Four-category ordinal scale; range = "no high school" to "college graduate"
Sex	Binary; female versus male
Immigrant status	Binary; settlers who immigrated after age eighteen versus Israeli-born and other immigrants

[a]Settler victimization scores (in this case ranging from 0—never—to 2—more than once) were averaged for each settlement. The individual settler's score was purged from the measure in order to reduce possible colinearity.
[b]STATEMENT: "Settlers should try to develop contacts with Arabs."
[c]STATEMENT: "There is a strong connection between the actions of settlers and the hastening of the messianic age."
[d]The individual settler's score is not included in his or her estimate. (see a above)
[e]This item refers to settlement anywhere in the West Bank or Gaza.

Table 5.2 Regression Analysis of Support for Vigilantism

Independent Variables	b	B^{a}	$p <$
Deviant Social Reaction Model			
Rationalizations for Vigilantism			
Individual victimization	.522	.23	.001
Settlement victimization	−.565	−.24	.001
Army base	.069	.03	.575
Arab vote	.140	.06	.184
Social distance	−.148	−.16	.002
Messianism	.124	.12	.018
Socialization to Vigilante Norms			
Group attitudes	1.676	.46	.001
Settlement size	−.003	−.10	.039
Leadership	−.342	−.11	.022
Years in settlement	.013	−.02	.624
Other Variables			
Settlement motivation[b]			
"Other motivations"	−.130		.447
"Rounded concerns"	.384		.073
"Self-interested"	.121		.543
"Gush Emunim values"	.208		.202
Religiosity	−.224	−.05	.281
Ethnicity	−.041	−.01	.777
Education	−.059	−.06	.231
Sex	−.081	−.02	.484
Immigrant status	.076	.03	.562

N of cases = 363   R Square = .330
F = 8.90, P < .001   Intercept = −3.410
Degrees of Freedom = 19

[a]Standardized regression coefficient.
[b]The overall dummy effect is not significant. The reference category is "Rabbi Kook followers."

Settlers claimed that they were influenced by the relative effectiveness of vigilante controls, and "settlement victimization" reflects, in part, the ability of vigilantism to deter Arab "deviance." After the influence of individual victimization is taken into account, high settlement victimization bares the ineffectiveness of vigilante behavior.[3] Those personally victimized experienced firsthand the failures of legal control. But where settlers saw that stoning incidents had become chronic, they lost confidence in the effectiveness of vigilantism. Vigilante actions were widely used as a strategy of control in the Gush Emunim community. Thus a high level of victimization implied a failure of vigilante controls.

In chapter 4 I noted that settler perceptions of the effectiveness of legal control were often independent of the actual intensity of legal responses to Arabs on the West Bank. In this light, it is not surprising that the availability of governmental social control in the settlements, as reflected by the presence of an army base next to an outpost,[4] did not significantly influence the extent of settler support for vigilantism.

I also noted earlier that settlers viewed vigilante violence as effective in part because it showed the power of Jewish settlement on the West Bank. Using variation in settler attitudes toward granting Arabs voting rights if the West Bank were annexed as an indicator of this dimension of vigilantism, a significant effect is not achieved (though in this sample opposed settlers are more supportive of vigilante actions). At the same time, the general attitudes of settlers toward Arab residents, as reflected by their willingness to develop future contacts with them, does have a statistically significant and strong influence upon settler support for vigilantism. Accordingly, though views on the failures of legal social control and the necessity of vigilante control were often unrelated to the actual intensity of Arab "deviance" or governmental responses, they were influenced by subjective attitudes about the nature of settler-Arab relations.

Settlers found support for the "legitimacy" of vigilantism in their views on self-reliance in Zionist action. One indicator of this dimension of settler rationalizations for vigilantism comes from settler beliefs concerning the role of settlement in the messianic process ("messianism"). Those who claimed that settlement actions have a direct and important influence upon the timing of the messianic age may be viewed as trusting more strongly in the efficacy of their own actions.[5] Clearly, settlers who believed that they could directly influence the divine order would be expected to support the usefulness of taking problems into their own hands. In fact, this measure of self-reliance has a statistically significant influence upon vigilante attitudes, though its impact is somewhat smaller than other significant variables reflecting settler rationalizations for vigilante activities.

Socialization to Vigilante Norms

Variation in the "costs" of vigilante violence are not reflected in this analysis since these were found to be uniformly low across the settlements during the period of study. At the same time, four additional measures that reflect the relationship between Gush Emunim settlers and the communities in which they live are taken into account. It was found in chapter 4 that settler vigilantism was a social reaction to deviance: a community-supported strategy of social control. Accordingly, we would expect that these settlement-settler variables would have an important impact on individual attitudes toward vigilantism.

These small intimate communities provide powerful socializing environments. Even for researchers in such settings there is a potential for "going native": of adopting the perspectives and attitudes of those who are the subject of study. These findings, in turn, support the view that the community plays an important role in fashioning individual attitudes toward social reaction. The level of support for vigilantism among others in an outpost is the most significant and powerful influence on individual vigilante attitudes in this analysis.

While this finding is consistent with our understanding of vigilantism as a form of deviant social reaction, it also presents a number of potentially confounding statistical problems. In the first case, we cannot be certain that this "group attitudes" measure reflects the socialization of settlers as opposed to the reputations of settlements. My qualitative interviews suggest that settlers did not choose outposts because of the nature of their vigilante reputations. Yet settlers were attracted to those settlements in which their overall worldview was reflected, and attitudes toward vigilante violence may in some cases have played a role in their settlement choice. Additionally, "group attitudes" may take on characteristics of unmeasured variables that have been excluded from the analysis. Thus they may be a misleadingly powerful influence in the regression. Though a residual analysis suggests that this problem is not a serious one,[6] again this possibility cannot be discounted altogether.

Perhaps the most serious potential danger of including a measure of "group attitudes" is that it would seriously alter the overall portrait of vigilante attitudes we gain in this study. Yet whether this measure is included or excluded, the influences of other factors remain relatively stable.[7] Accordingly, though this finding is presented with some reservations, the weight of evidence suggests that it is a valid indicator of the importance of community norms in developing individual attitudes in the settlements, and one that does not lead to serious biases in our overall understanding of vigilantism.

Two other measures that reflect the extent of the community's influence upon individual settlers—"settlement size" and "leadership"—also have statistically significant, though smaller, influences upon attitudes toward vigilantism. Smaller communities, where face-to-face interactions are more frequent, have been found to exert greater informal pressures toward conformity than larger communities (Schwartz, 1954). Following this, the analysis indicates that settlers who lived in the smallest settlements were more supportive of vigilante actions. They were, in this sense, less able to deviate from the predominant community norms that supported vigilantism as a strategy of deviant social control.

Those who had held important leadership positions in the settlements were less supportive of vigilantism than other settlers. While this finding is on its face inconsistent with my view of socializing pressures toward support for vigilantism, it may reflect a very different type of socialization. Leaders in the settlements were exposed more often than other settlers to outsiders who were concerned about the consequences of vigilante behavior. They were responsible for defending the settlement enterprise and its actions to the government and the general Israeli public. Perhaps it is precisely because leaders had greater contact with and sensibility toward outsiders who opposed vigilantism that they were also less influenced by the normative climates of these vigilante communities.

One measure that also reflects socialization processes—

"years in settlement"—does not have a statistically significant influence upon vigilante attitudes. The length of time
settlers lived in the West Bank did not influence their overall
support for, or opposition to, vigilante behavior. In this regard,
we may speculate that it does not take very much time in
these intense and small communities to become identified
with perspectives that are seen as central to their survival.

The Influence of "Other" Variables

While measures drawn from my discussion of deviant social
reaction have important impacts on settler attitudes, variables
that reflect other explanatory models for differentiating support for vigilantism are not found to be important in this
analysis.

A number of observers have argued that Gush Emunim's
generally negative attitudes toward Arabs have laid the foundations for settler violence in the West Bank (e.g., see Rubinstein,
1982; Shafir, 1985). Thus we might expect that settlers who
came to the settlements more ideologically attached to Gush
Emunim would be more supportive of vigilante actions. This
perspective is not supported in this study. Using settlement
motivation clusters developed in chapter 3 as an indicator of
attachments to Gush Emunim, no statistically significant effect is found. We might speculate accordingly that settler vigilantism has its origins in contacts between Jews and Arabs in
the West Bank rather than in the ideological development of
the Gush Emunim movement.

The religious and ethnic backgrounds of settlers have also
been identified as sources for anti-Arab violence. Israelis
whose origins lie in the Islamic countries are seen as less
tolerant of Arabs (e.g., Weller, 1974; Shipler, 1987). Religious
Gush Emunim supporters have in turn been linked to the
view that Arabs must, like the biblical Canaanites, choose to
"accept Jewish rule, or fight" (Lustick, 1987:124). Once we
control for the social reaction components of vigilantism, we
find that these ethnic and religious differences do not account
for significant variation in settler perspectives on vigilante
violence.

Social status has been identified more generally as an important element in the development of vigilantism (e.g., Sederberg, 1978), though the nature of its overall relationship to crime and deviance has recently been questioned (e.g., Glaser, 1979; Tittle et al., 1979; Braithwaite, 1981). In the Gush Emunim settlements, status, as measured by educational achievement (or ethnic origins[8]), did not significantly influence settler support for vigilante actions.

Finally, little difference is found between men and women in the settlements, and between those who grew up in Israel and those who immigrated as adults, in their support for vigilantism. Though, as noted in chapter 4, women are less likely to act as vigilantes, they show no less or greater support than men for this strategy of deviant social control. In turn, though immigrants have been identified both as radicals and moderates in the Gush Emunim settlements (Waxman, 1985), this analysis suggests that, at least in terms of their vigilante attitudes, they are similar to their native-born or Israeli-educated peers.

Explaining Vigilante Behavior

Vigilante settlers acted as agents of the Gush Emunim community. They carried out a strategy of social control that was widely discussed and broadly supported in these settlements (see chapter 4). Accordingly, variables examined in the discussion of vigilante attitudes would be expected to have a very different impact upon reported vigilante behavior. In this case the major concern is not with the normative climate that legitimates vigilantism, but rather to identify those characteristics that lead a community to enlist certain of its members to act as agents of community social control.

I begin with characteristics that reflect a settler's relative social position within a settlement (Table 5.3). Here those traits that make a settler an appropriate candidate for the vigilante role are examined. I then turn to the social locations of settlers within the wider Gush Emunim community. Here the

Table 5.3   Variables Examined in Analysis of
Vigilante Behavior[a]

Variable

The Vigilante as Agent of Community Social Control

Social Position
 Leadership
 Sex
 Immigrant status
 Individual victimization

Social Location
 Settlement size
 Settlement victimization
 Year of settlement
 Army base

Other Variables
 Settlement motivation
 Religiosity
 Messianism
 Ethnicity
 Education
 Social distance
 Arab vote
 Support for vigilantism

[a]For measurement of variables, see Table 5.1.

concern is with the extent to which settlements "need" to enlist their members for vigilante actions. As with the analysis of support for vigilantism, these measures, as well as other variables that reflect alternative models of vigilante behavior, are examined in the context of one general multivariate model (Table 5.4).

Because of the difficulty in ranking the relative seriousness of different forms of vigilantism and the fact that many of those settlers admitting vigilante behavior did not report its type, the different forms of vigilantism evidenced in the settlements are not distinguished. Rather, the likelihood of settler participation in vigilante activities is examined. With the exception of "roadblocks," which generally involved much less serious law violations than other vigilante acts, all of the behaviors listed in Table 4.5 are included in this analysis. Thus settler actions that range from the destruction of Arab prop-

Table 5.4　Logit Regression of Vigilante Behavior

Independent Variables	b	p <
The Vigilante as Agent of Community Social Control		
Social Position		
Leadership	1.463	.001
Sex	1.954	.001
Immigrant status	−1.480	.001
Individual victimization	.940	.025
Social Location		
Settlement size	−.012	.035
Settlement victimization	1.307	.005
Year of settlement	.111	.181
Army base	−.731	.079
Other Variables		
Settlement motivation[a]		
"Other motivations"	−.786	.151
"Rounded concerns"	−.507	.401
"Self-interested"	−.908	.231
"Gush Emunim values"	−.136	.780
Religiosity	.393	.520
Messianism	.187	.258
Ethnicity	−.351	.428
Education	−.230	.129
Social distance	.052	.691
Arab vote	−.056	.866
Support for vigilantism	.454	.024

N of Cases = 435
Intercept = −13.074
Chi square = 131.89, P < .001

[a]The overall variable effect is not significant. The reference category is "Rabbi Kook followers."

erty to actual and threatened physical violence against Arabs are examined.

Discussion of the relative importance of variables will center upon probability estimates associated with changes in the values of independent measures. Such comparisons are easily interpreted and consistent with the logistic regression format necessitated by this analysis.[9] Though these probabilities could have been estimated at any point in the distribution of vigilante behavior, they refer here to changes in the likelihood of vigilantism when the overall probability of vigilante behavior is otherwise 50 percent (Table 5.5).[10]

Table 5.5   Selected Probability Estimates for
Significant Variables

Variable	Probability Estimates[a]
Leadership	
Held leadership post	.81
Other settlers	.50
Sex	
Male	.88
Female	.50
Immigrant Status	
Immigrated as adult	.50
Other settlers	.19
Individual Victimization	
Never	.50
One or more times	.72
Settlement Size	
16	.45
40	.38
70	.30
100	.23
132	.17
Group Victimization	
0.00	.50
0.75	.73
1.75	.88
Support for Vigilantism	
Strongly disagree	.61
Disagree	.71
No opinion	.80
Agree	.86
Strongly agree	.91

[a]These estimates refer to the case where a settler's overall
probability of involvement in vigilante behavior is 50 percent
(before inclusion of the independent variable examined). Thus
the logit response function is approximated by setting the
value of xb at 0 and allowing only the variable being estimated
to vary $(xb = 0 + b_i x_i)$.

The Vigilante as Agent of Community Social Control: The Role of Social Position

Vigilante actions were seen by settlers to play an important
part in their overall security. This aspect of vigilantism, cou-
pled with possible legal sanctions and potential Arab reaction
against the settlements, made vigilantism a particularly sensi-

tive community matter. It was to be handled by those in responsible positions, both because it was an important aspect of community life and because it could have significant impacts upon these settlements. Though leaders were found to be less supportive of vigilantism than other settlers, their leadership roles make them, for this reason, appropriate candidates for participation in vigilantism. And indeed, leaders were significantly more likely to report involvement in vigilante actions than other settlers (Table 5.4). Having occupied a leadership post increased a settler's absolute estimated probability of vigilante involvement by more than 30 percent (Table 5.5)

We have seen that settler vigilantism is often carried out as a small military operation. The "paramilitary" aspects of such vigilante activities, in turn, should make women less appropriate candidates for the vigilante role, even though they were no more or less supportive of vigilante actions than men. Their roles in society generally, and in the military in particular, give them little responsibility for activities involving force and violence. Moreover, in those settlements that were governed by traditional religious principles, it was unlikely that women would be seen as appropriate candidates for armed actions against neighboring Arab villages and towns. In fact, the differences found in bivariate distributions of vigilante behavior are supported in this multivariate analysis. Women, all else being equal, were much less likely than men to become involved in vigilante behavior.

The measures "immigrant status" and "individual victimization" reflect the voluntaristic aspects of social position, and both contribute significantly to this analysis. Immigrants had a special status in these communities. These settlers were known to be "activists," people who could be called upon when the community was in trouble. Their decision to immigrate at a time when comparatively few Jews had chosen to come to Israel further reinforced their image as men and women willing to come to the community's aid. Their estimated likelihood of involvement in vigilantism, in turn, was some 31 percent greater than that of settlers who grew up in Israel.

Whether a settler was victimized in a stoning incident also influenced his or her likelihood of being called to serve as a vigilante. Victimization gave the settler a personal interest in vigilantism that was recognized by others in the settlements. Again, this identified the settler as an appropriate candidate for vigilante actions. Though the effect of "individual victimization" was somewhat smaller than that of other variables discussed, those settlers who had been victimized in a stoning incident were significantly more likely to report involvement in vigilante behavior.

The Vigilante as Agent of Community Social Control: The Role of Social Location

The social location of settlers within the Gush Emunim communities was linked to the opportunity structure of vigilantism. For smaller settlements to bring to bear a similar quantity of social control as larger ones, a larger proportion of settlers needed to be called. Thus "settlement size" would be expected to and does have a direct influence upon the probability of settlers being involved in vigilante actions. When settlers who lived in the smallest settlements are compared with those from the larger outposts, a 28 percent difference in probability estimates is found.

"Settlement victimization" also reflects this aspect of social location. Accordingly, in settlements where settlers were more likely to encounter stoning incidents, there should have been a greater need for individuals to be enlisted in the vigilante role, even though, as we saw earlier, high victimization represents a failure of vigilante controls. And indeed, this measure has the largest effect of any variable in the analysis. Taking into account other relevant factors, those who lived in settlements where other settlers had on average been victimized more than once, as compared with settlers in outposts with little victimization, were almost 40 percent more likely to be involved in vigilante activities.

The number of years a settler had lived in these West Bank communities was also examined as an element of the opportunity structure of vigilantism. Since vigilante actions were seen by most settlers as an appropriate and legitimate response to Arab "harassments," those who had lived longest in the settlements would be expected to have a greater likelihood of involvement in vigilantism. Perhaps reflecting the relatively short time that most settlers have lived in these outposts, this measure does not significantly influence reported vigilante behavior (though in this sample involvement is slightly higher among veteran settlers).

Location next to an army base provides the final measure of social location. Settlers argued that vigilantism developed because of the failures of legal controls in the West Bank. Accordingly, we would expect that the immediate presence of army resources would make it less likely that individual settlers would need to be enlisted as vigilantes. The presence of a military base, of course, also reflects the heightened possibilities for apprehension and sanction by military personnel. Again, though in the expected direction, location near an army base did not have a significant impact upon vigilante actions. We may speculate here that the general support for vigilantism that settlers claimed came from army personnel would offset some of the effects that derive from the availability of official legal control agents.

The Effects of "Other" Variables

Other scholars suggest that vigilantes may be distinguished from ordinary citizens in the community by their relative conservatism in values and attitudes (e.g., Kreml, 1976). Little support is found in this analysis for this perspective. Settlers who came to the Gush Emunin outposts because of attachments to the conservative political and religious philosophies associated with Gush Emunim were not more likely than others to participate in vigilantism. Nor were less-religious settlers, or those with weaker attachments to the messianic aspirations associated with Gush Emunim, significantly less likely to become involved in vigilante actions, though the latter group was significantly less supportive of vigilantism than were other settlers.

Socioeconomic status has also been identified as an important focus of inquiry in examining participation in vigilantism (Sederberg, 1978:301). As in the analysis of vigilante attitudes, the influence of social status is assessed by examining both the educational achievements of settlers ("education") and their "ethnicity." Again no significant influence of status upon vigilante behavior is found once aspects of social location and position of settlers are accounted for.

The political goals of social-group-control vigilantism (Rosenbaum and Sederberg, 1976:12–17) are reflected in the general attitudes of settlers toward West Bank Arabs. While these might be expected to influence settler involvement in vigilantism, settlers who wanted fewer contacts with Arabs, as well as those who were against granting West Bank Arabs voting rights, evidenced no greater likelihood of vigilante actions.

Finally, general settler "support for vigilantism" is included in the analysis.[11] We would clearly expect that, all else being equal, a settler's opposition to or support for vigilantism as a control strategy would influence his or her willingness to participate in vigilante violence. Though vigilante attitudes do significantly influence vigilante behavior, the range of probability estimates for this measure is only 30 percent. Thus gender differences, settlement size and victimization, leadership, and immigrant status all have similar or stronger impacts on the likelihood of vigilante involvement than a settler's relative support for vigilante actions.

Can We Generalize from the Israeli Case?

The social-control rationalizations used generally in the settlements to defend settler violence also explain variation in settler support for vigilantism. Thus concerns with the failures of legal controls and the legitimacy and effectiveness of vigilante violence significantly influence vigilante attitudes. The normative climates supporting vigilantism within the settlements also have important impacts upon vigilantism. Those settlers who came from outposts where others were less sup-

portive of vigilantism, or larger settlements where the influence of settler norms were weakest, as well as those most
exposed to the competing norms of outsiders opposed to vigilante violence were found to be less supportive of vigilante
actions.

Actual settler involvement in vigilantism is explained primarily by the appropriateness and necessity of enlistment in
the vigilante role. Leaders in the settlements, male settlers,
immigrants, settlers victimized more often, and those who
come from smaller or more victimized outposts were all more
likely to report acting as vigilantes. Their social roles in society generally, their positions in the settlements, their identifi-
cation as potential volunteers, and the extent to which settlements were "in need" of their services were all important
factors in explaining their participation in vigilante behavior.
Even when less disposed toward vigilantism than other settlers, as were settlement leaders, these prerequisites of the
vigilante role led to a greater likelihood of vigilante actions.

These data thus provide strong support for using a model of
deviance as social reaction for understanding vigilantism in
the Gush Emunim settlements. But it might be argued that
these findings are likely to be specific to the Israeli scene. As
noted in chapter 2, the Gush Emunim settlements have grown
out of a special set of religious and Zionist ideals particular to
Jewish settlement in Israel. The complicated political status
of the West Bank, as well as a large Israeli military presence in
the region, also set this case apart from many others. Yet,
evidence from vigilantism in other settings lends support to
the more general relevance of my findings.

The importance of the failures of legal control in rationaliz-
ing vigilantism is recognized in a number of other studies.
Brown notes, for example, that American vigilantism generally arose as a response to "the absence of effective law and
order" in frontier regions (1975:96). Similarly, Little and Sheffield found in their comparative study of American and English vigilantes that vigilantism tends to arise in regions un-
dergoing social upheaval, where legal controls are weak or
unavailable (1983).

While the failures of legal control are linked to vigilantism by other scholars, we need not assume that vigilante violence emerges only where there are no agents of legal authority. American vigilantism had an important "symbolic value" for Western settlers independent of its crime control functions (Brown, 1975). Thus American vigilantes, like those on the Israeli frontier, often acted when they were near to established legal institutions. As Caughey notes, the San Francisco vigilante committees "rose up alongside regular courts and in defiance of them" (1957:221).

The role of legitimacy in the development of vigilantism is apparent both in the United States and the Canadian Yukon. In Canada, the introduction of the Mounted Police effectively put an end to vigilante actions, even though legal control was in many ways less successful in responding to problems of crime and disorder than was vigilantism (Stone, 1979). In the Yukon, vigilantism was seen as a competing and illegitimate strategy of social control. In contrast, in the United States, where there was a long tradition of self-reliance (Little and Sheffield, 1983), vigilantism was seen as complimentary to the established legal system (Brown, 1971). Indeed, Americans felt no "less public spirited" in participating in vigilantism than they did in supporting legal responses to criminal behavior (Brown, 1976:108–9).

Findings as regards the relationship between socio-economic position and vigilantism and the importance of leaders in the development of vigilante violence are consistent with observations made in historical analyses of vigilantism. In the case of English Private Prosecution Societies in the eighteenth and nineteenth centuries, for example, there was comparatively little systematic relationship between social class and vigilante involvement (Little and Sheffield, 1983:799). At the same time, "prominent members" of these vigilante Societies held leadership positions in the larger community. Social position was also an important aspect of American vigilantism. Brown (1976:104–5) notes that a number of prominent community leaders became involved in vigilante committees in the American West.

In the case of contemporary vigilante committees in Peru, the vigilante plays a formal role as an agent of deviant social reaction. Here the appropriateness of enlistment for vigilante actions has unambiguous boundaries. Villagers not "eligible" for vigilante service include those under eighteen and over sixty years of age, as well as women and the ill (Gitlitz and Rojas, 1983). These villagers, like women in the Gush Emunim settlements, are not appropriate candidates for the vigilante role. Peasants in Peru who do not appear for vigilante duty, or who show up drunk or unprepared, are formally sanctioned by other villagers:[12]

> (They) are initially admonished and then either fined or assigned additional tasks, most often extra nights patrolling. In many hamlets one of the tasks assigned to women is that of enforcing discipline, and they have been known to drag recalcitrants from bed. (Gitlitz and Rojas, 1983:186)

The Vigilante and the Community

There is, as documented above, considerable evidence suggesting that a model of deviance as social reaction is appropriate for explaining vigilantism in other settings. Yet it should be noted that this perspective on vigilantism is very different than that developed in other studies. Unlike traditional approaches that emphasize the broad historical, political, psychological, or social causes of vigilante violence (e.g., Skolnick, 1969; Brown, 1971; Kreml, 1976; Rosenbaum and Sederberg, 1976), this model emphasizes the role of vigilantism as a community-supported strategy of social control and the vigilante as an agent of the community.

Nowhere is this contrast greater than in the portrait of individual vigilantes presented by other scholars (e.g., Kreml, 1976; Sederberg, 1978). Vigilantes are often pictured as "deviants" within their own communities; as isolated and extreme figures who are driven to vigilante violence. As William Kreml remarks in his essay on "The Vigilante Personality":

He (the vigilante) is a conservative personality at heart but, more important, he is a frightened personality, unable to understand the problems that social unorthodoxy, change, and racial or ethical differences have brought upon him.

When activating circumstances of temporary instability and threat occur within a community, persons who possess the kinds of traits identified here often approach the threshold of vigilante activism. The interplay of social stress and certain psychological characteristics of the vigilante personality forge an alloy of vigilante behavior which is ready to wreak vengeance upon the community and its people. (1976:63)

My analyses suggest that support for and participation in vigilante actions are more strongly linked to the "division of social control labor" (Griffiths, 1984) in vigilante communities than to characteristics that are seen to predispose particular individuals to vigilante violence. Indeed, Gush Emunim vigilantes are seen in their settlements as upstanding community members, as loyal volunteers who heed the community's call even when they are less supportive than others of vigilante violence.

6

Potential Antigovernment Violence

We saw in chapter 2 that Gush Emunim's roots lie in norms that forbid a withdrawal from any part of the Land of Israel. The Gush Emunim movement emerged when these rules were challenged. The settlements of Gush Emunim developed as a strategy to prevent what settlers defined as potential government violations of these norms. While social reactions to Arabs became an increasingly important part of settlement life, the question of potential reactions against the Israeli government remained at the core of the settlement enterprise.

Before the Camp David agreements with Egypt, the supporters of Gush Emunim were able to counter government actions against settlement with strategies of social control that involved little physical violence. But the presence of Jewish settlements had not ensured Israeli sovereignty in the Sinai Peninsula. Nor had illegal settlement actions stopped the withdrawal from that region. As a result, the prospect that illegal settlement attempts and protests would not be enough to counter a similar government action in the West Bank became very real to Gush Emunim settlers after the Sinai experience. The possibility of armed reactions to "governmental deviance" suddenly became a subject of great seriousness and frequent discussion throughout the Gush Emunim outposts.

In this chapter, general settler support for norms that define the Israeli government as deviant is examined. Settler views on what constitutes governmental deviance are then compared with settler support for antigovernment violence. A surprising degree of dissonance is found between the intensity of settler definitions of deviance and their views on the legitimacy of violent forms of social reaction. Multivariate regression analyses are used to explain this contradiction in settler attitudes. These analyses show that social networks constrain settler reactions to behavior they define as deviant. They suggest more generally that the definition of deviance should be conceptually distinguished from the sanctions used for its control.

Definitions of Deviance

As discussed in chapter 2, settlers use two normative systems to support their view that the West Bank must not be relinquished. In the first case, they rely upon religious rulings that place retention of the West Bank in the strictest category of Jewish law. The *Halachah* generally puts the sanctity of human life above religous norms. The individual is allowed to transgress the religious obligation if human life is at stake. But the rabbis of the Gush Emunim movement argued that the *Mitzvah* to retain the West Bank is a commandment *Ye'Horeg Va'Al Ya'Avor:* one for which an individual is obligated to be killed rather than transgress.

Support for this particular view of Jewish law was wide ranging in the Gush Emunim settlements. When asked whether they believed that withdrawal from Judea and Samaria falls under the principal of *Ye'Horeg Va'Al Ya'Avor,* almost three-quarters of the settlers agreed or strongly agreed (Table 6.1). Support for this definition of the *Halachik* importance of retention of the West Bank was found in all of the settlements studied. A plurality of settlers in every outpost supported the view that the dictum *Ye'Horeg Va'Al Ya'Avor* applies to Jewish sovereignty in the West Bank (Table 6.2).

The extent to which settlers defined government attempts to restrict settlement as unacceptable may also be seen in settler

Table 6.1   Settler Agreement that *"Ye'Horeg Va'Al Ya'Avor"* Applies to the West Bank

STATEMENT: "It is forbidden under any conditions to withdraw from Judea and Samaria as the dictum *Ye'Horeg Va'Al Ya'Avor* is applicable."

Response	(%)
Strongly disagree	4.4
Disagree	11.7
No opinion	9.9
Agree	22.6
Strongly agree	51.4

Number of cases = 491

Table 6.2   Percentage Support for Applying *Ye'Horeg Va'Al Ya'Avor* to the West Bank (by settlement)

Settlement	Strongly Disagree	Disagree	No Opinion	Agree	Strongly Agree	N
Atzmona	0%	13%	6%	13%	69%	16
Beit Choron	4	12	8	28	48	25
Beit El	16	16	26	16	26	19
Beit El Bet	8	15	12	15	50	26
Beit Yatir	0	27	5	36	32	22
Carmel	0	15	0	15	70	13
Chadasha	20	10	0	10	60	10
Elon Moreh	4	8	8	20	60	25
Kaddumim	0	4	11	21	64	28
Karnei Shomron	3	3	0	33	60	30
Kfar Adumim	11	21	7	29	32	28
Kfar Tapuach	0	6	0	28	67	18
Kochav HaSchachar	14	18	4	21	43	28
Mevoh Dotan	0	17	6	28	50	18
Michmash	21	8	17	29	25	24
Mispe Yerecho	4	21	17	25	33	24
Neve Tzuf	0	15	11	30	44	27
Ofra	0	14	17	21	48	29
Sheve Shomron	0	9	9	32	50	22
Shilo	0	14	14	24	48	21
Tekoah	0	23	0	8	69	13
Yakir	8	16	4	16	56	25

comparisons between the right to settlement on the West Bank and the general right of Jews to immigrate to Israel. This right of immigration (*Aliyah*) forms one of the major tenets of modern Zionism. In the 1930s, British actions to restrict immigration sparked violent resistence to British rule (Bell, 1977). Many settlers responded to questions regarding withdrawal from the West Bank by asking how other Israelis would react to withdrawal from Tel Aviv or Jerusalem. As one settler argued when asked whether a democratic vote against settlement would change his view that the government does not have a right to compromise on the future of the West Bank: "Would you ask this from a Tel Avivian? If the majority of the nation decides to give up Tel Aviv, what will you say? . . . These are not issues which may be decided by the majority or democracy!"

More than eight of ten settlers who responded to this item agreed that stopping *Aliyah* and forbidding settlement on the West Bank are equivalent actions (Table 6.3). In turn, though more than half the settlers strongly agreed that a "government decision to forbid settlement in Judea and Samaria is similar in seriousness" to stopping immigration to Israel, only 2 percent strongly disagreed. Support for defining restrictions on settlement as deviant because they "violate" Zionist principles is again found throughout the settlements studied (Table 6.4). While there is variation in the extent of support for this

Table 6.3 Equating Stopping *Aliyah* with Stopping Settlement on the West Bank

STATEMENT: "A decision by the government to forbid Jewish settlement in Judea and Samaria is similar in seriousness to a decision to forbid *Aliyah* to the Land of Israel."

Response	(%)
Strongly disagree	2.0
Disagree	7.6
No opinion	3.9
Agree	27.3
Strongly agree	59.2

Number of cases = 493

Table 6.4   Percentage Support for Equating Stopping *Aliyah* and
Restricting West Bank Settlement

Settlement	Strongly Disagree	Disagree	No Opinion	Agree	Strongly Agree	N
Atzmona	0%	0%	0%	40%	60%	16
Beit Choron	0	18	0	36	46	22
Beit El	0	11	21	26	42	19
Beit El Bet	0	7	0	30	63	27
Beit Yatir	0	13	4	26	57	23
Carmel	0	0	0	36	64	14
Chadasha	9	18	0	36	36	11
Elon Moreh	0	0	4	16	80	25
Kaddumim	0	7	4	18	71	28
Karnei Shomron	7	0	0	35	59	29
Kfar Adumim	7	14	7	36	36	28
Kfar Tapauch	6	17	6	11	61	18
Kochav HaShachar	0	7	0	32	61	28
Mevoh Dotan	22	11	0	44	22	18
Michmash	0	22	17	13	48	23
Mispe Yerecho	0	8	8	38	46	24
Neve Tzuf	0	14	4	29	54	28
Ofra	3	3	3	27	63	30
Sheve Shomron	0	9	9	22	61	23
Shilo	0	10	0	30	60	20
Tekoah	0	0	0	53	47	15
Yakir	0	8	4	24	64	25

perspective, in every settlement a large majority of settlers equated actions against settlement with a decision to forbid *Aliyah* to the entire Land of Israel.

Attitudes Toward Antigovernment Violence

Restrictions on Jewish settlement on the West Bank or attempts at a territorial compromise in the region violate strongly held religious and Zionist norms in the Gush Emunim community. Indeed, there are few norms defined in Jewish law or within the modern Zionist context as seriously. But what of settler reactions to potential or actual governmental "deviance"?

Most settlers supported protest actions when the interests of the settlements were threatened.[1] Yet only a third of the Gush Emunim settlers were involved in demonstrations or settlement actions in which there were "violent" conflicts with the army or police (Table 6.5), and of these more than three-quarters claimed to be involved in only "passive resistance."[2] Only 8 percent claimed to have participated in some type of "active" resistance to the government. Accordingly, a minority of settlers had been involved in incidents they themselves defined as involving violence, and the majority of this group did not "actively" resist government reactions to the settlers.

What of the extent of these "violent" incidents? As was noted in our review of the history of Gush Emunim, there were few cases of actual physical conflict between settlers and the military. The small number of settlers who claimed to be injured as a result of Gush Emunim actions, in turn, further illustrates the relatively mild context of these "violent" incidents.[3] Only 1 percent of settlers surveyed received any injuries as a result of conflicts with the government, and only one settler claimed to have received an injury that required hospitalization.[4]

It might be argued that the absence of serious violence between settlers and the Israeli government was due in large part

Table 6.5   Participation in "Violent" Demonstrations or Settlement Attempts

QUESTION: "Have you ever been involved in a demonstration or settlement attempt in which settlers came into conflict (literally "violence") with the police or the army?"

Response	%
No	63.3
Yes, passive resistance	28.4
Yes, active resistance	8.3

Number of Cases = 500

to the fact that there were no systematic government attempts to relinquish sovereignty over regions of the West Bank. The relatively small number of settlers involved in conflicts with the government may, in turn, be attributed to the fact that the majority of the settlements were established with government support. Thus settler reactions to governmental "deviance" may have included little violence because the "infractions" of the government were comparatively mild. What would occur if settler values concerning settlement were challenged more directly?

Settlers were surveyed as to whether they agreed that resistance must only be passive if the government begins to uproot Jewish settlements in the West Bank.[5] While slightly more than 40 percent of settlers disagreed with this view, and thus advocated active resistance to governmental "deviance," almost half agreed that only passive resistance would be acceptable (Table 6.6). Indeed, fewer than 14 percent of settlers surveyed disagreed strongly that only passive resistance must be used, while over 20 percent agreed strongly with these sentiments. Looking at the individual settlements, we find a degree of dissension about the legitimacy of active resistance to the government that is in sharp contrast to settler consensus over definitions of governmental deviance (Table 6.7). In turn, in only five of the Gush Emunim outposts did the majority of settlers oppose the use of only passive resistance to the government.

Table 6.6   Support for Only Passive Resistance

STATEMENT: "Only passive resistence would be legitimate in opposing a government attempt to dismantle settlements in Judea and Samaria."

Response	%
Strongly disagree	13.3
Disagree	29.5
No opinion	8.4
Agree	28.0
Strongly agree	20.8

Number of Cases = 488

Table 6.7   Percentage Support for Only Passive Resistance (by settlement)

Settlement	Strongly Disagree	Disagree	No Opinion	Agree	Strongly Agree	N
Atzmona	0%	13%	13%	53%	20%	15
Beit Choron	5	15	5	40	35	20
Beit El	11	21	11	32	26	19
Beit El Bet	15	31	0	23	31	26
Beit Yatir	0	50	9	18	23	22
Carmel	21	43	7	21	7	14
Chadasha	0	27	18	36	18	11
Elon Moreh	4	32	12	28	24	25
Kaddumim	29	36	7	11	18	28
Karnei Shomron	13	57	7	13	10	30
Kfar Adumim	0	29	0	43	29	28
Kfar Tapuach	22	28	6	22	22	18
Kochav HaShachar	7	21	4	46	21	28
Mevoh Dotan	6	31	13	25	25	16
Michmash	9	17	17	30	26	23
Mispe Yerecho	13	17	13	42	17	24
Neve Tzuf	18	18	11	39	14	28
Ofra	20	17	7	37	20	30
Sheve Shomron	4	35	9	30	22	23
Shilo	5	30	10	30	25	20
Tekoah	13	13	20	47	7	15
Yakir	12	20	8	32	28	25

Before turning to the general problem of why settler reactions are not uniformly more serious (given the particular religious and Zionist norms of settlers) it is important to define the extent of potential settler violence against the government. Earlier conflicts were described by settlers as including active "violent" resistance to the military. Yet, as already noted, these for the most part resulted in only a small number of minor injuries to settlers. In their responses to this item in the survey, are settlers referring to more serious acts of violence? Or would active "violent" resistance against government attempts to dismantle settlements in the West Bank follow the pattern of earlier Gush Emunim protests?

In qualitative interviews, settlers predicted that resistance to a withdrawal from the West Bank would include much more serious acts of violence than had been used in previous Gush Emunim actions. One settler described the potential reactions of her neighbors to a government attempt to uproot that settlement in the following manner:

> I don't like to talk about that possibility. I hate the thought of contemplating it—if the government would do that. It's a nightmare! But there are people I know here who would fight until they have no bullets left. They would have to be taken out wounded or in a casket. . . .

Another settler, when comparing the reactions of Amanah settlers to others in the West Bank, gave a similar picture of potential settler violence:

> Definitely the Amanah settlers would be the ones to fight. I don't think everyone in Beit Choron would fight and maybe everybody in Ofra would and everybody in Elon Moreh would. But in most of the settlements, not everybody would fight. But in all the Amanah settlements, there would be people who would.
>
> (What would be your reaction?)
>
> I don't know. Perhaps it's better to take a plane out of Israel and leave, or else fight. I don't know. I don't know how to fight. I don't think I would stay in Israel.

In the view of yet another settler, acts of violence would come long before the uprooting of settlements. In response to a question about his reaction to Shimon Peres assuming the Prime Ministership and proposing a territorial compromise in the West Bank, he argued:

> It's allowable for him to do that. From a legal aspect it's allowable for him to make that decision. . . . I don't know what I would do (in response to this decision). I am a very passive type of person. I hope someone will shoot him. Someone else will shoot him with a rifle . . .

that is what will happen. I am almost certain. There are in the settlements enough crazies . . . not many but we have them. There are enough people in Samaria that are ready to kill Peres if he does something like this. . . . Also Begin if he does this. I do not believe that he will be here a week after he makes that decision.

Though a number of settlers thus support antigovernment violence if a withdrawal from the West Bank is attempted, it is surprising—given the intensity of settler norms concerning sovereignty over the West Bank—that such a large number of settlers support only passive resistance to government actions to uproot settlement. Why is there such disproportion in settler attitudes?

Examining Variation in Deviance Definition and Control

To answer this question, the factors that underlie the intensity of settler definitions of governmental deviance are compared with attitudes toward antigovernment violence. My concern is with the characteristics that explain why settlers define potential government actions as less or more deviant, and how these differ from those that identify settlers who are most or least willing to support strategies of active social reaction. Initial findings show that there was much less agreement within these communities about how to respond to government violations of Gush Emunim norms than how those norms themselves should be defined. Now the question is whether there are significant differences in the ways in which these attitudes toward deviance definition and control are developed.

As in chapter 5, these questions are explored using multivariate regression techniques. In this case a series of explanatory variables that would be expected to influence settler understandings of governmental deviance and its control are included (Table 6.8).

Table 6.8 Description of Variables

Variables	Measurement
Connections to Gush Emunim	
Yeshiva background	Binary; has not attended higher *Yeshiva* versus others
Settlement motivation	Five categorical variables (see chapter 3)
Messianism	Five-category ordinal scale, range = "strongly disagree" to "strongly agree"[a]
Social Networks	
Year of settlement	Interval scale; range = 69–82
Immigrant status	Binary; settlers who immigrated to Israel after age eighteen versus Israeli-born and other immigrants
Ethnicity	Binary; "Western" versus North African/Middle Eastern origins
Socialization	
Group attitudes	Interval scale, range = 6.86–9.0[b]
Leadership	Binary; other settlers versus those who have served as "Settlement Secretary" or "Chair of Secretarial Committee"
Social cohesion	Ordinal scale; range = 8.0–20.0
Other Variables	
Education	Four-category ordinal scale; range = "no high school" to "college graduate"
Religiosity	Binary; Sabbath-observant settlers versus others
Sex	Binary; female versus male

[a]STATEMENT: "There is a strong connection between the actions of settlers and the hastening of the messianic age."
[b]The individual settler's score is purged from the measure.

Perhaps the most important of these are measures that assess the connections of settlers to the Gush Emunim movement. We would expect, all else being equal, that those who studied in the rabbinical academies from which Gush Emunim grew, as well as those who came to the Gush Emunim settlements more strongly attached to Gush Emunim ideals, would respond to future violations of Gush Emunim norms more seriously.

The role of social networks in the development of settler

attitudes is also examined. Donald Black argues that there is substantial evidence supporting the proposition that governmental social control is unlikely to be exercised against "intimates" (1976:41). Here I question whether deviant social controls are similarly influenced by social networks. Such ties between settlers and Israeli society generally are reflected in the length of time settlers have lived on the West Bank, their "immigrant status," and their ethnicity.

The isolation of the settlements from the rest of Israeli society—a result of both their geographic isolation and the danger of travel through Arab villages and towns—meant that over time settlers became less "intimate" with Israelis that lived within Israel's 1967 boundaries. Immigrants were also less likely to have strong ties with Israelis outside the settlements. They were not educated in Israel's public school system and generally had fewer family links in the country. Nor were they likely to have served in Israel's regular army, a major socializing institution in Israeli society. In contrast, Jews of North African or Middle Eastern descent generally had stronger ties both to their extended families and the "Oriental" community as a whole.

As in chapter 5, the influence of socialization processes in the settlements is taken into account. In these models, though, settlement size is excluded because of its contribution to instability in regression estimates,[6] and a measure of social cohesion is included. A number of scholars have linked social solidarity to deviant behavior, arguing that deviance plays an important role in developing a sense of community among members of a society (e.g., Durkheim, 1933; Coser, 1963; Erikson, 1966; Lauderdale, 1976). Here I question whether settlers who feel more strongly and positively linked to others in their settlements are likely to have different perspectives on "governmental" deviance and its control than other settlers.[7]

Three other demographic characteristics—education, religiosity, and gender—of settlers are included. These are significant factors in many aspects of social life and thus are usefully examined in analyses of settler perspectives on deviance and social reaction.

Definitions of Deviance

As we saw above, settlers used two distinct normative systems to define government actions against Jewish settlement in the West Bank as deviant. In the one case they relied upon Zionist norms that demand free immigration of Jews to the Land of Israel. In the other, they followed religious rulings that forbid any territorial compromise in Judea and Samaria. In this analysis these two dimensions are combined into one overall measure of settler definitions of deviance.[8] Table 6.9 presents basic results.[9]

Table 6.9 Regression Analysis of Definitions of Deviance

Independent Variables	b	B[a]	PR<
Connections to Gush Emunim			
Yeshiva background	.646	.14	.008
Settlement motivation[b]			
"Rabbi Kook followers"	−.256	−.05	.274
"Other motivations"	−.405	−.10	.054
"Rounded concerns"	−.017	−.00	.953
"Self-interested"	−.927	−.16	.002
Messianism	.244	.15	.003
Social Networks			
Year of settlement	−.025	−.03	.476
Immigrant status	.269	.05	.217
Ethnicity	.229	.05	.285
Socialization			
Group attitudes	1.785	.28	.001
Leadership	.300	.07	.155
Social cohesion	.063	.08	.086
Other Variables			
Education	−.091	−.06	.235
Religiosity	.188	.03	.574
Sex	.024	.00	.902

N of cases = 439
$F = 7.95, P < .001$
Degrees of Freedom = 15
R Square = .220
Intercept = −6.476

[a]Standardized Regression Coefficient
[b]The overall dummy effect is significant at p < .05. The reference category is the "Gush Emunim values" cluster.

The most important dimension for explaining these settler attitudes is represented by attachments to Gush Emunim and its values. Thus we find that those who attended rabbinical academies associated with the Gush Emunim movement were significantly more likely than other settlers to define government actions to curtail or uproot West Bank settlement as deviant. Clearly, these centers of religious learning were successful in presenting their particular view of the role and importance of Judea and Samaria in Jewish law.

Those settlers who came to the West Bank because of commitment to more general values of the Gush Emunim movement were also significantly more supportive of these definitions of governmental deviance. Using settlement motivation clusters developed in chapter 3, it was found that settlers who placed ideology before self-interest (in choosing to live in the West Bank) were more likely, later on, to define government actions against settlement as more serious. Of all the groups, those who came to the settlements in order to improve their quality of life were least supportive of views that defined the government as deviant.

Belief in the connection between West Bank settlement and the fulfillment of the messianic process also significantly influenced settler attitudes toward "governmental deviance," just as it served to reinforce the opposition of Rabbi Kook and his students to any territorial compromise in these areas (see chapter 2). Settlers who agreed that "there is a strong connection between the actions of settlers in Judea and Samaria and the hastening of the messianic age" were more likely than others to see any attempts to disrupt West Bank settlement as unacceptable.

While variables reflecting connections to Gush Emunim and its values have a strong influence upon settler definitions of deviance, those that assess their social network ties to Israeli society are not important in understanding settler attitudes. Immigrants were neither less nor more supportive of these deviance definitions than those who grew up in Israel, even though their ties to other Israelis were certainly weaker than Israeli-educated settlers. Nor were newcomers to the settlements or those whose families originated in North Africa or the Middle East—all likely to have stronger ties—any less supportive of such definitions.

As in chapter 5, these small and intimate communities are found to provide powerful socializing environments. The most important individual influence in this analysis is produced by the group attitudes measure. The greater support existing in a particular outpost for these definitions of deviance, the more likely is the individual settler to support them. Yet we are again faced with the statistical problems inherent in using a collective score to predict individual attitudes.

In this analysis the group attitudes measure corrects directly for the potential biases that might result from settlers choosing outposts because they reflect their ideological orientations.[10] But even if this correction does not completely address the statistical questions raised by this measure, as in the previous chapter, its inclusion in the analysis does not introduce substantial changes to the regression model as a whole. Indeed, the portrait of deviance definitions that we would gain had this item been excluded is not altered appreciably by the inclusion of the group attitudes item.[11]

Other socialization measures—"leadership" and "social cohesion"—do not significantly influence definitions of deviance in this sample. Yet the latter variable has a larger (b = .083) and statistically significant effect[12] when we examine an uncorrected stratified sample of settlers. Such a sample emphasizes the differences between the settlement communities, giving approximately equal weight to small and large settlements. Using this sample we find that settlers who are more strongly attached to others in their settlement are more willing to define government actions as deviant.

Why should attitudes toward community life affect attitudes toward deviance?[13] In the Gush Emunim outposts these definitions represent community sentiment. More than this, they are a crucial part of the founding ideology of Gush Emunim and its settlements. Settlers who are more strongly attached to their settlements are thus likely as well to become more attached to these core community concerns.

Of "other" measures, none have a significant effect upon settler definitions of governmental deviance. Thus differences of religious observance, gender, and education do not directly influence settler support for these deviance definitions when other factors measured are accounted for.

Attitudes Toward Social Reaction

In assessing settler attitudes toward reactions to governmental "deviance," the analysis is similar to that employed in the previous section. Two differences here are the inclusion of the definitions of deviance measure as an explanatory variable and the inclusion of a group-attitudes item for passive resistance. Group attitudes are measured in this analysis using a dichotomy.[14] In this way, those settlements that generally support passive resistance are differentiated from others. The measure of social reaction is the "passive resistence" item discussed earlier in the chapter (see Table 6.6). The basic findings from the regression are reported in Table 6.10.

Of those variables reflecting a settler's connections to Gush Emunim, only messianism retained its importance in this analysis. *Yeshiva* background, an important factor in predicting how settlers perceived governmental deviance, had no significant impact upon support for active resistance. Indeed, while small, the direction of this effect is reversed from the previous analysis. Those with a higher *Yeshiva* education show a slightly greater advocacy of passive resistance. "Settlement motivation," in turn, though also an important factor in explaining deviance definitions, has only a small and insignificant influence upon the type of resistance settlers see as appropriate.

"Messianism" retains its strong and statistically significant effect. Yet, in this case, we may attribute these findings not so much to settler links to Gush Emunim as to their views on self-reliance. In analyzing vigilante attitudes, it was found that settlers who felt their settlement actions were influencing the messianic process had a special sense of the extent to which their behavior could deter Arab "harassments." Given the findings as regards "settlement motivation" and higher *Yeshiva* background, it is likely that this factor, rather than

Table 6.10 Regression Analysis of Passive Resistance

Independent Variables	b	B[a]	PR<
Connections to Gush Emunim			
Yeshiva background	.070	.02	.716
Settlement motivation[b]			
"Rabbi Kook followers"	−.140	−.04	.451
"Other motivations"	.171	−.05	.307
"Rounded concerns"	−.129	−.03	.572
"Self-interested"	.095	−.02	.677
Messianism	−.142	−.11	.028
Social Networks			
Year of settlement	.072	.12	.010
Immigrant status	.299	.07	.084
Ethnicity	.400	.11	.019
Socialization			
Group attitudes	.393	.26	.001
Leadership	.054	.02	.749
Social cohesion	.020	.03	.497
Other Variables			
Education	.067	.05	.275
Religiosity	.095	.02	.725
Sex	−.021	−.01	.894
Definitions of deviance	−.064	−.08	.086

N of cases = 435
F = 5.08, *P* < .001
Degrees of Freedom = 16
R Square = .163
Intercept = −2.585

[a]Standardized Regression Coefficient
[b]The overall dummy effect is not significant. The reference category is the "Gush Emunim values" cluster.

attachments to Gush Emunim, is responsible for the significance of the "messianism" measure.

While connections to Gush Emunim lose their importance in this analysis, the effects of social networks grow considerably. The number of years settlers lived on the West Bank had a strong and significant influence upon their support for active resistance. Indeed, this is the second most important variable in the analysis. Settlers who had lived in the West Bank longer were much more supportive of active resistance to governmental "deviance" than newcomers to the region.

Those of European descent were also more supportive of active resistance. Thus Jews of Middle Eastern or North African descent—who had more traditional extended family ties within Israel—were more likely to oppose active resistance, even though they were no more or less supportive of the deviance definitions examined earlier. While "immigrant status" does not quite reach the criteria for statistical significance ($p < .05$), those settlers in the sample who were educated in Israel were also less supportive of active resistance.

Of socialization measures, only group attitudes had a significant influence upon settler support for active social reaction. In those outposts where there was an environment supportive of active resistance, individual settlers showed much stronger support for antigovernment violence. While qualitative interviews suggest that settlers do not choose outposts because of their commitment to active or passive resistance,[15] as in the earlier models I examined whether the inclusion of this settlement level measure appreciably altered the overall picture of settler attitudes. Again, there is little substantive change when this measure is excluded.[16]

Settler definitions of deviance did not play a significant role in explaining variation in attitudes toward social reaction. In order to examine this surprising result more carefully, the individual effects that the religious or Zionist dimensions of deviance definition had upon settler attitudes toward active resistance were measured independently. Examining the problem in this way, it was found that Zionist norms do not significantly influence attitudes toward social reaction. But religious norms have a moderate and significant effect. Just as religious norms were most instrumental in the development of Gush Emunim, they are those most likely to contribute to support for serious antigovernment violence.

While religious norms significantly influence settler views on social reaction, differences in religious observance per se do not. As in the prior analysis, neither religiosity, education, nor gender had a significant impact upon settler support for active resistance once connections to Gush Emunim, socialization, and social networks had been accounted for.

The Constraints of Social Networks

We can now return to our original problem. Government threats to West Bank settlement were defined by the vast majority of Gush Emunim settlers as among the most serious violations of religious and Zionist norms. Yet most settlers claimed they would not support serious antigovernment violence even if the government were to uproot settlements. How can we explain this contradiction between the intensity of settler definitions of attempts to restrict settlement and the mildness of sanctions they are willing to bring to control this "offending" behavior? The answer lies in the differences evidenced in regression analyses of deviance definition and social reaction.

Settler definitions of deviance relate directly to their connections with the Gush Emunim movement. In the Zionist rabbinical academies, settlers learned of the primacy of aspects of religious law. They became schooled in those beliefs which would come to define actions against settlement as deviant. Settlers more strongly attached to the ideals that lay at the core of Gush Emunim were also more likely to define government actions as unacceptable when they were compared to settlers whose settlement motivations were personal or self-interested. The view that West Bank settlement plays an important role in the redemptive process also increased settler commitment to the notion that actions threatening to the settlements represented serious normative violations. Those settlers who believed the redemptive process would be hindered by threats to settlement were those more likely to define government actions as deviant.

While settler beliefs about what constitutes governmental deviance were strongly related to the institutions and ideals that sparked the Gush Emunim movement's development, settler ties to Israeli society generally played a much more important role in explaining their potential reactions to the government. Settlers with stronger connections to other Israelis were less sympathetic of more extreme reactions, and those with fewer family and friendship ties tended more often to support active resistance. This is not to say that any of these groups identified government actions as less or more deviant. Rather, the social networks connecting some of these settlers to other Israelis made it harder for them to conceive of deviant social controls that would involve serious violence.

Indeed, in the case of those settlers who studied in a rabbinical academy, we found a direct contradiction between their attitudes toward governmental deviance and its control. Higher *Yeshiva* background increased a settler's likelihood of defining government actions against a settlement as unacceptable. This because rabbinical institutions played a major role in defining the religious norms that forbid territorial compromises in the West Bank. But in these same *Yeshivot*, settlers also learned of the importance of the bonds that tie all Jews together as brothers.[17] And thus they were slightly less likely (in this sample) to advocate more serious violence against the Israeli government.

A more concrete example of this tension was found in observations of those settlers who went to the Sinai Peninsula to prevent its return to Egyptian control. Many believed that the area near Yamit was a part of the Land of Israel. Thus for them, the principle of *Ye'Horeg Va'Al Ya'Avor* applied directly to the Sinai settlements in the Yamit region. While these settlers spoke with passion about the importance of retaining Jewish sovereignty over the Sinai, they were equally passionate about not spilling Jewish blood.

These settlers were seen by many in the West Bank as the most ideological and committed of Gush Emunim supporters. But they followed the teachings of rabbis from the Merkaz HaRav *Yeshiva* in Jerusalem who argued that violence against other Jews was totally unacceptable. Accordingly, these settlers, who were more likely than others in the Gush Emunim outposts to define actions against settlement as deviant, were also less likely to advocate violent resistance against the government. Their connections with traditional religious authority, which on the one hand reinforced their definitions of governmental deviance, were also responsible for emphasizing the bonds that unite all Jews as a nation. These latter networks reduced the potential for serious antigovernment violence.

For settlers generally, there were strong social networks

that bound them to the rest of Israeli society. Those ties continued to be reinforced by army service, work, and family within Israel's 1967 boundaries, as well as strong religious connections with the rest of Jewish society in Israel. Settler definitions of government actions and their strategies of reaction to the government were thus "out of line" in the Gush Emunim settlements at the time of this research because the networks binding Gush Emunim settlers to other Israelis remained relatively strong.

Distinguishing Between Deviance and Social Reaction

My discussion of settler definitions of government deviance and attitudes toward social reaction relates to a more general problem in the study of deviant behavior. Beginning with the development of the labeling approach to deviance in the early 1960s, scholars began to define deviant behavior primarily in terms of the reactions of society (e.g., Kitsuse, 1962; Becker, 1963; Kitsuse and Cicoural, 1963; Erikson, 1966). This approach, which quickly became predominant among sociologists (Spector, 1976), emphasized the fact that there is considerable disagreement within a society about what norms should be enforced or indeed what society's rules should be.

For deviance theorists, the most important variable in defining deviant behavior became the societal reaction itself. As Donald Black argues: "Deviant behavior is conduct that is subject to social control. In other words, social control defines what is deviant. And the more social control to which it is subject, the more deviant the conduct is" (1976:9). Such an approach avoided a major weakness of earlier theories. They had failed to recognize the fact that individuals who carry out similar normative violations may be treated quite differently. As Kai Erikson explained: "It is an easily demonstrated fact . . . that working class boys who steal cars are far more likely to go to prison than upper class boys who commit the same or even more serious crimes, suggesting that from the point of view of the community lower class boys are somehow more deviant" (1962:308).

This examination of the Gush Emunim settlers also suggests that similar norms may be enforced in very different ways depending on the connections of the community to those who are defined as deviant. But these results illustrate, as well, the importance of distinguishing between deviance and social reaction. While social networks constrain reactions to deviance, they do not affect the way deviance is defined. It is not because many settlers defined the government as less deviant that they were unwilling to contemplate serious antigovernment violence. Rather, they were unwilling to use such violence against those to whom they were strongly bound.

7

Conclusions

I began this book by identifying a type of rule-violating behavior that has often been ignored in the study of deviance. Most research in this field has focused upon social or sexual outcasts, or "common" criminals. Strict boundaries have been placed between the behaviors that characterize deviance and those that characterize social control. In this study our attention turned to a very different type of deviance. It was called "deviant social reaction" because the examined behaviors violated the rules and laws of the general society and were at the same time collective efforts to uphold rules and values advocated by a subcommunity in that society.

The Gush Emunim settlements provided a unique opportunity to study deviant social reactions. The outposts examined were small, geographically isolated communities that afforded an unusually controlled and manageable natural environment where attitudes toward deviance and strategies of deviant social control were developed. I was also able to examine different forms of deviant social reaction, as settlers of Gush Emunim were involved in evading and resisting society's rules in order to control both the Israeli government and West Bank Arabs.

In this study a detailed analysis of the dynamics of deviant social reaction in the Gush Emunim settlements was presented. The development of these reactions, as well as the substantial variation that existed among settlers in evaluating and sanctioning behavior they defined as deviant was explored. Below the basic contributions of this research to the study of deviance and social control are summarized. The implications of these findings for future Jewish settler violence in the West Bank are also examined.

Contributions to the Study of Deviance

In the public mind, deviants are often pictured as offenders driven to rule-violating conduct. They are the products of disorganized communities and broken homes. They are tempted into a world outside the boundaries of acceptable conduct by questionable associations or illicit desires. While deviance is often viewed by laymen as irrational behavior, among scholars there has been a general movement that identifies rule-violating conduct as purposeful and rational (Clarke and Cornish, 1985). Indeed, though there are important exceptions (e.g., Wilson and Herrnstein, 1985), the image of a "reasoning criminal" most closely approximates recent criminological concern with the origins of deviant behavior (Cornish and Clarke, 1986a). The portrait of deviance gained from this study of the Gush Emunim settlements provides additional evidence for this emerging perspective on the rationality of crime and deviance. Yet it also challenges the relatively narrow view of criminal motivation and decision-making that has characterized recent studies.

Scholars have been struck by the commonplace, almost routine calculations that make up most criminal decisions (e.g., Cornish and Clarke, 1986b; Felson, 1987). They have thus tended to focus upon "limited" or "minimum" standards of rationality (e.g., Carroll and Weaver, 1986; Feeney, 1986; Walsh, 1986), presenting offenders who make calculations about personal gain and risk quickly, and often without very much sophistication. These are essentially "selfish" criminals. As Hirschi and Gottfredson note, their crimes are motivated simply "by the self-interested pursuit of pleasure and the avoidance of pain" (1987:959). In contrast to these approaches, study of deviant social reaction points to an "altruistic" rationality for deviance, and a normatively based criminal decision-making process that has more in common with the complexity of societal reactions than the mundane character of most criminality.

The roots of Gush Emunim's deviant social reactions were traced to a subcommunity within Israeli society with a special outlook on the nature of Israel's future and the rules under which Israel should be governed. Gush Emunim drew its support from a new religious Zionist generation in Israel which argued that religious legal considerations must have a direct influence upon every area of public policy and public life in the Jewish state.

Rabbinical authorities most influential with this new generation of religious Zionists ruled that it was forbidden under any circumstances to relinquish Jewish sovereignty over any part of the Land of Israel. They told their students and followers that they must be willing to sacrifice their lives rather than allow a withdrawal from the West Bank. They created the potential for deviant actions on the part of Jewish settlers by defining any government behavior that threatened Jewish control over the West Bank as deviant.

For settlers, support for these norms developed from their attachments to the ideals of the Gush Emunim movement, the institutions from which those ideals developed, and their socialization to communities where support for defining government restrictions on settlements as deviant were strongest.[1] For them, violations of governmental rules were neither routine nor self-interested. Indeed, they were connected to the cataclysmic events of the millennium and their commitments to the wider communities with which they identified.

My examination of vigilantism also points to the altruistic rationality of settler crimes. Settler vigilantism was purposeful and strategic. Settlers did not excuse their criminal behavior, rather they defended it much as reactions to deviance are rationalized and defended in the larger society. They claimed that vigilantism arose from their concern with the failures of legal social control. They defended vigilantism in reference to its effectiveness and costs, arguing that it was a powerful tool in preventing Arab "deviance" and one that led to few reactions on the part of the Israeli government. When explaining the particular strategies of control they employed, settlers found legitimacy for vigilantism by referring to sanctions the Israeli army used against Arabs on the West Bank.

It might be argued that settlers were merely "neutralizing" their own deviance (Sykes and Matza, 1957) by constructing an elaborate and contrived defense for those whose authoritarian personalities and violent tendencies led them to vigilante violence (e.g., Kreml, 1976; Sederberg, 1978). Yet, examination of variation in settler participation in vigilante actions further supports this view of an altruistic rationality for settler criminality.[2] The selection of vigilantes in the Gush Emunim community points both to calculation in the choice of those best able to serve the community and the willingness of settlers to act on the community's behalf.

Settler involvement in vigilantism was explained primarily by the appropriateness and necessity of enlistment into the vigilante role. The settler vigilante took upon himself a responsibility that derived from his position in the settlements or society generally. He was likely to act in settlements which showed a greater "need" for vigilante actions. In turn, even when less supportive of vigilantism than other settlers, those who fulfilled these characteristics of the vigilante role were more likely to become involved in vigilante violence.

Study of deviant social reaction thus suggests that scholarly concern with the "reasoning criminal" should include altruistic as well as self-interested components of rationality. The view that deviants "seek to benefit themselves by their criminal behavior" (Cornish and Clarke, 1987:933) does not recognize that deviance is often intended to defend much broader interests of family or community (see also Black, 1983; Wheeler et al., 1988).[3] Moreover, the routine characteristics of those crimes that have occupied a central place in recent criminological research have hidden from view the complexity which underlies much deviant conduct (see also Wheeler et al., 1988).

Contributions to the Study of Social Control

Because the deviance examined in this study was also a form of social reaction, this research allowed a view of social-control behavior that is often unavailable in conventional studies. Paul Rock notes that scholars concerned with societal reaction tend to oversimplify the complexities of the social-control process (1974:144–45). In part this is due to the often overwhelming processes of social control that are part of large-scale society. In contrast, a direct and immediate relationship between individual attitudes and community reaction was identified in the Gush Emunim settlements. As a result, my analyses yielded important insights into the ways in which perceptions of deviance and social control influence the form and intensity of community reactions to deviance.

One of the more established propositions in the study of social-control states is that legal control will develop in direct proportion to the failures of informal control systems (e.g., Schwartz, 1954; Black, 1976). Implicit in this proposition is the assumption that the success or failure of social control is an objective fact, and thus we may examine changes in social control systems without reference to the social psychology of the persons who create those systems. While it is certainly attractive to develop propositions about social life without reference to the often erratic attitudes of human actors (e.g., Black, 1976; Stark, 1987), my research implies that we cannot understand the development of social control without reference to definitions of deviance.

Settler perceptions of the effectiveness of governmental social controls in the West Bank, and not the objective amount of that control, were most important in determining the emergence of vigilante behavior. Settler vigilantism replaced governmental responses not necessarily because the strategies of control employed by the Israeli military were ineffective, but rather because settlers disagreed with the military's definition of what behaviors demanded a societal reaction. Moreover, in the eyes of many settlers, vigilantism was necessary, however aggressive the government response. For them, Arab residents of the West Bank would either lose respect for settlers unwilling to take care of their own problems, or would not take seriously agents of control who did not come from the settlements.

Accordingly, it is difficult to speak of the development of alternative control systems without reference to the very subjective views of those who decide upon and carry out social-control behaviors. Evaluations of social control, like those of deviance itself, are very much a product of human perceptions (e.g., Becker, 1963). While it would be useful if we could predict the development of alternative control systems from objective factors only, my research suggests that the filter of human evaluations cannot be disentangled from the broader social-control process.

My findings also shed light upon the entanglements between definitions of deviance and societal reaction. Scholars have come to define deviance primarily in reference to the reactions of the community. Examination of deviance definitions and attitudes toward social reaction in the Gush Emunim settlements suggests that scholars should more carefully distinguish between behaviors frowned upon in the community and the sanctions brought against those defined as deviants.

Government threats to settlement were defined by the vast majority of Gush Emunim settlers as among the most serious deviant actions because they violated both religious laws and Zionist beliefs. Yet most settlers would not support serious antigovernment violence even if the government were to uproot settlements. This disproportion in settler attitudes was explained with reference to the social networks that tied settlers to the larger society. These networks did not affect the way settlers defined deviance. Rather, they constrained settlers' willingness to carry out serious antigovernment violence.

The Future of Jewish Settler Violence

This study of deviant social reaction has a number of troubling implications for the future of Jewish settlement in the

West Bank and the ability of the Israeli government to respond to and control settler deviance. These derive in part from a developing isolation of settlers from other Israelis, as well as recent Palestinian rebellion against Jewish rule in the West Bank and the responses of the Israeli military to Arab protests and stone-throwing.

Since this research was conducted, the isolation of West Bank settlers from other Israelis has been growing. The development of employment opportunities in the settlements, the movement of extended families to these outposts as they became more comfortable places to live, and a tendency for male settlers to serve their reserve duty in special regional patrols in the West Bank have all contributed to a breakdown of strong ties between these settlers and Israelis who live within the pre-1967 boundaries of Israel. The increasing danger of traveling through Arab areas has also significantly diminished the extent to which settlers are a part of the larger Israeli community.

My findings suggest that the potential for serious antigovernment violence will grow as the social networks tying settlers to other Israelis become weakened. This potential is, of course, heightened further by the pressures for territorial compromise in the West Bank which have developed as a result of increasing Palestinian unrest in the region. The norms for serious antigovernment violence have always been present in the Gush Emunim movement, though the constraints of social networks and the absence of territorial concessions have led to little actual conflict. With these latter restraints removed, it is likely that the uprooting of settlements will be accompanied by violent armed resistance on the part of some, and perhaps many, Jewish settlers.

There is also strong reason to suspect that the violence settlers direct at West Bank Arabs will become more serious in the coming years. In the past, settlers have found legitimacy for destroying Arab property and detaining and sometimes beating Arab villagers from actions of the Israeli military. Israel's recent policies in response to the Palestinian rebellion in 1988 cannot but lead settlers to rely upon more violent vigilante actions than had typified the community-supported

control strategies described in this study.[4] The Israeli government's initial decision to respond to stone-throwing with gun-
fire, and its attempt later to reduce the death toll by encourag-
ing "beatings" (rather than shootings) of rioters (Fisher, 1988),
will certainly be used by settlers to support the legitimacy of
more violent vigilante actions.

And what of potential government reaction to the settlers
themselves? My research indicates that legal authorities find
it difficult to effectively respond to deviant social reaction. In
part this results from the collective nature of this deviance.
Law violators are shielded by the communities in which they
live. Indeed they are agents of control of those communities.

But difficulties in responding to settler deviance also derive
from the similarities between deviant social reactions and legal
controls. Settlers rationalized and explained their criminality
in reference to concepts of legitimacy and effectiveness which
are well-accepted in Israeli society. In the case of vigilantism,
they claimed that they acted in support of the established order.
In the case of antigovernment violence, they argued that they
were supporting the true Jewish values of Zionism. While settler behavior might violate the formal boundaries of societal
norms, this research implies that the wider society is likely to
be inconsistent and confused in its effort to sanction and control crime that is normatively justified and carried out by those
who do not fit stereotypes of deviance or criminality.

My findings do not provide an optimistic view of the future
of Jewish settler violence in the West Bank. But they appear
consistent with a more general trend among Israeli Jews and
Palestinian Arabs to use the language of deviance to define the
problems of coexistence in the Land of Israel. For both peo-
ples, there is a growing concern with gaining the status of
victim and defining their violence as social reaction. As the
Israeli philosopher David Hartman observed in the winter of
1987 after a series of violent confrontations between the Israeli army and West Bank Arabs:

> The only thing to come out of these demonstrations so
> far is that each side is fighting to be perceived by the
> world as the true victim. Neither one is looking at the

other and saying, "How do we resolve this moral dilemma in a way that will create dignity and space for each of us?" All that you have here is a politics of reaction, not a politics of vision. (Friedman, 1987b)

Notes

Chapter 1

1. While definitions of deviance vary from study to study, as Sagarin (1975, 1985) notes, they have in common a concern with activities that are viewed as negative or unacceptable by the general community.

2. A lack of interest in using themes relating to deviance may be attributed both to the different concerns of those who study social movements and the general failure of the sociology of deviance to attract interest in other areas of sociology.

3. This is not to say that social scientists have ignored the perspectives of those labeled as deviant. Indeed, much attention has been paid, especially since the emergence of the societal reaction perspective, to the worldview of deviant individuals (e.g., Reiss, 1961; Becker, 1963). Yet there is in this research generally a tendency to draw distinct lines between the ideas presented by these deviants and those developed in the context of societal reactions (e.g., Sykes and Matza, 1957). Also, there are few treatments of this problem as it relates to the case of political deviance.

4. It should be noted that the norms or rules upheld by the deviant group may be advanced as well in some form in the general society. This is the case, for example, with super patriots, and is applicable to many aspects of the Gush Emunim phenomenon (see chapter 2).

5. The term "subcommunity," as it is used here, refers to a group within a society with a set of shared values or rules that sets it apart from others and allows the development of some type of collective action. In this sense, the term may refer to any of a number of social units, from ethnic or political groups to small towns or villages. For a suggestion that deviance theory may be applied to all these different types of communities, see Erikson (1966:9).

6. A review of articles listed under the deviance subject area in sociological abstracts shows that Liazos's observation about the sociology of deviance has not changed a great deal since the early 1970s.

7. As is the case with much of international terrorism.

8. Schafer, for example, develops the category of the "pseudo-convictional criminal," in order to distinguish those offenders who act for "selfish" reasons, and thus corrupt an "otherwise honorable dispute over the pluralistic nature of values" (1971:386).

9. It might be argued that the larger Gush Emunim movement (dis-

cussed in chapter 2) would provide a broader view of the Gush Emunim community than its settlements. Yet is is extremely difficult to define this community empirically since Gush Emunim has never established any official membership lists. In contrast, the Amanah settlements provide a clearly identifiable group of settlers that have chosen to be formally identified with Gush Emunim and its special views on the nature of Israel's future.

10. Some seventy-five settlements existed or were under construction in the West Bank by 1982 (Benvenisti, 1982). While many of these have been associated with the Gush Emunim movement, either because of the membership of Gush Emunim leaders in these outposts or the participation of Gush Emunim in their founding, only the settlements studied had chosen to be formally identified with the Gush Emunim movement.

11. See Newman (1985) for a discussion of the new settlement models developed in the West Bank.

12. Indeed, in a few settlements settlers blocked government efforts to erect security fences, primarily because they wanted to be viewed like other Israeli communities (not as residents in a hostile foreign environment).

13. Because these settlers were in charge of the settlements' everyday dealings with outsiders, it was decided that they were the natural choice for "official" interviews in the settlements. The role of *Mazkir* differed slightly from settlement to settlement. In most cases, the *Mazkir* performed a function similar to that of a mayor in a small town. In a few settlements, though, the *Mazkir* was more of a paid functionary than active leader.

14. In fifteen of the settlements, the *Mazkir* was interviewed. In two settlements, interviews were conducted with the head of the "secretarial committee," and in one smaller settlement, three settlers participated with the *Mazkir* (a newer member) in our discussion. In one outpost, a member of the "secretarial committee" was interviewed.

15. In three cases (Atzmona, Neve Tzuf, and Kfar Tapuach) the settlements were in the midst of serious internal problems during the research period or the settlement leaders were called for military reserve service or to other responsibilities. As a result, settlement leader interviews were not conducted. Instead, discussions with "ordinary" settlers, the survey (see below), and secondary sources were used to gather information on settlement history and policy.

16. The success of the survey may be due in part to the fact that there was no attempt to elicit formal permission from the settlements. Had that been done, there would probably had been much more difficulty in gaining access to settlers, as well as some censorship of sensitive questions.

17. Settlement size varied from under twenty to over 100 families (Table 1.1).

18. For the fourteen settlements with thirty or more households, one settler from each household was asked to complete the written survey. The choice of whether a husband or wife was chosen (almost all households

included married couples) was determined for the most part by who was approached first, or less frequently by who preferred to fill out the survey. When one sex began to predominate in the researcher's sample, he or she then tried to have the "undersampled" sex respond in future households. In any case, because men were less likely to be at home during the early evening hours, when the survey was conducted, they were slightly underrepresented in the sample (43 percent versus 57 percent).

For those settlements with twenty or fewer households, every settler at home was approached to be surveyed. In the three settlements with between twenty and thirty households, researchers were encouraged to obtain fifteen responses in the half of the settlement assigned to them.

19. Fluctuations in the number of responses in each settlement were related both to the size of the settlement and the response rate itself. In one settlement, for example, less than twenty settlers were surveyed. This was due to the fact that this was both a very small settlement (twenty families) and one in which a number of settlers still spent much of their time in nearby Jerusalem. Nonresponses resulted primarily from settlers' not being at home during the time the survey was administered. On average, fewer than three settlers in every outpost refused to fill out the questionnaire, and of these most claimed that they were going out or were too busy.

20. The Lebanese War did not relate directly to the primary regional concerns of the Gush Emunim settlers. Nor did it pose a direct threat to the security of the West Bank region. Indeed Israel referred to the War in its opening days as a *Miftzah* or "operation," implying that it was similar to other Israeli actions against Palestinians in Lebanon.

Chapter 2

1. There is, in fact, considerable disagreement among both secular and religious scholars concerning the actual boundaries of the Land of Israel (Shilhav, 1985). This lack of consensus does not apply to the West Bank region, which has a central place in the biblical narratives, and was not a part of the State of Israel before 1967.

2. The Sinai figures prominently in the biblical description of the Jewish Exodus from Egypt. The Golan Heights contained a large Jewish population from the first century until the Moslem conquests.

3. The question of the final disposition of the territories captured in 1967 grew into a major political issue and foreign-policy problem. The conflict in Israel was never to center upon the legitimacy of Israel's claim to the occupied lands. Even the ruling Labor government, while calling for "territories for peace," acknowledged that Israel had the "right," for historical and security reasons, to claim these territories. Rather, the conflict was to be between those who called for the actual fulfillment of Jewish "rights" in these areas and those who argued that it was neither desirable because of

demographic and moral concerns, nor possible for political reasons (if Israel hoped to gain a peace treaty with its Arab neighbors and retain American support) for Israel to retain all of these regions.

4. At present, Israeli courts are only obligated to follow the *Halachah* in cases involving family law. In other areas of law, judges often choose to refer to Jewish legal concepts and rulings, but they are not bound by them. For an interesting discussion of the role of *Halachah* in modern Israel, see Abramov (1976).

5. Many of these were *Yeshivat Hesder*, where young men studied and completed their army service at the same time. This is in marked contrast to the pattern set at "non-Zionist" rabbinical academies, where most students request deferments from army service.

6. In Israel, there are two Chief Rabbis, one for Jews of Ashkenazi or European origin, and one for those whose backgrounds lie in North Africa and the Middle East. The latter group includes Jews in Europe who trace their ancestry to the Spanish expulsion of 1492.

7. For a description of Rabbi Kook's writings in English, see Zinger (1972).

8. Quotations that are not cited in the text are drawn from in-depth interviews conducted as part of this study.

9. On the Passover holiday in 1968, a group led by followers of Rabbi Kook rented a hotel in Hebron after their requests for settlement in the city had been denied. The government had rejected their requests because of its policy of excluding settlement in heavily populated regions of the West Bank. When the settlers refused to leave Hebron after the Passover holiday, the government took no action to remove them. Fearful of public reactions led by the Whole Land of Israel Movement, the government eventually compromised with the settlers and agreed to the establishment of a Jewish city to be built on the outskirts of Hebron. The settlement, to be called Kiryat Arba, became the largest and most controversial Israeli outpost on the West Bank built before the 1973 war.

10. Shortly after the 1967 war, a group of noted Israelis from varying political backgrounds established the movement which dedicated itself to annexation of the occupied territories (Isaac, 1976). The group generally avoided actions that might embarrass the Israeli government.

11. A large parchment scroll containing the Pentateuch.

12. In order to form a government, Begin joined forces with the Democratic Movement for Change, a short-lived political party that did not sympathize with the goals of Gush Emunim.

13. In earlier illegal settlement attempts, there were large numbers of Gush Emunim supporters, but few intended to actually settle at the sites (e.g., at Masudiyah in December 1975).

14. The army gave them the "minimum help" they needed to survive as a settlement: "They (army officers) could not see little kids living in conditions without water and electricity" (from an interview with the settlement secretary at Shilo).

15. While evictions had been carried out at Jericho and Dotan, these did not involve any serious conflicts.

16. One of these was a settlement revolving around a rabbinical academy. This group, which had come to Beit El from Ofra, eventually decided to form its own independent settlement.

17. This point was made during interviews of a number of settlement leaders. For example, the settlement secretary of Mispe Yerecho argued: "Gush Emunim does not in fact exist." Interestingly, the movement continued to be cited by the press as an active force whenever former Gush Emunim leaders were involved in protest actions.

18. This estimate is gained from my survey of Gush Emunim settlers.

Chapter 3

1. The typology is based on a statistical clustering technique described in Note 5.

2. Estimates of settler characteristics presented in the text or in tables are "weighted" to correct for the stratification of the survey and the over-representation of women in the sample (see chapter 1, note 18).

3. In the case of settlers in Atzmona, the items were altered to reflect settlement in Gaza or Sinai.

4. A series of items were listed under under one question: "What role would you say each of the following played in your decision to move to a settlement in Judea and Samaria?" Settlers were given the choice of listing each motive as "predominant," "important," "didn't play role," or "discouraged decision."

5. Cluster analysis is used to place "objects," in this case individual settlers, into groups "suggested by the data, not defined a priori, such that objects in a given cluster tend to be similar to each other in some sense, and objects in different clusters dissimilar" (SAS, 1982:417). This analysis was done using the SAS FASTCLUS procedure.

6. An additional cluster containing approximately one percent of the settlers was also found when developing these groups. Because of the small size of this cluster, it is excluded from the following analyses.

7. Characteristics of settlers in each cluster were compared to the overall weighted frequencies for the entire sample. In this way, the observed frequencies within each cluster were tested against the expected frequencies suggested by the sample.

8. In the open-ended interviews, a number of settlers reported that they came to the settlements as a result of strong friendship or family ties with other settlers.

9. These included: Secretary for Internal Affairs, Secretary for External Affairs, Treasurer, Chair of the Secretarial Committee, Member of the Secretarial Committee, Head of the Absorption Committee, Member of the Absorption Committee, Member of the Educational Committee, Member of

the Culture Committee, Member of the Religion Committee, Member of the Activity Committee, Representative to Amanah, Representative to Yesha, Representative to the Regional Council.

10. While there have been large meetings and Gush Emunim "clubs" or regional chapters, from the outset the movement has preferred not to establish any official membership lists. According to Sprinzak (1981), this is part of a strategy used by Gush Emunim's leaders to exaggerate public support for the group.

11. One exception was Beit El Bet, which was established as a *Yeshiva* community. Policy here is set by the Rabbinical authorities in the settlement.

12. Smelser defines a value-oriented movement as a "collective attempt to restore, protect, modify, or create values in the name of a generalized belief" (1962:313). This definition is clearly applicable to the Gush Emunim movement in its initial years.

Chapter 4

1. According to the 1980 census, there were 704,000 Palestinian Arabs living in the West Bank. This figure excludes East Jerusalem, which was annexed after the 1967 war.

2. As the situation of Atzmona is similar to that of the West Bank Gush Emunim settlements, survey results from that outpost are included in the findings reported in this chapter.

3. For example, the establishment of Kaddumim in 1975 led to anti-Israeli demonstrations and riots in most West Bank Arab towns (Ma'Oz, 1984:124).

4. Friedman notes that the maximum penalty "for throwing a stone at another person" in the West Bank is twenty years in prison, "just five years less than the average murder sentence in Israel" (1987a:16).

5. This item was phrased in the language settlers used to defend vigilantism in qualitative interviews. It should be noted that there is no Hebrew term for vigilantism.

6. This question was not included in the original survey instrument. For the first eleven settlements surveyed, researchers took with them this item written on a separate sheet. When they picked up the survey they would show the question and ask the settler to write the answer out of view of the researcher. This method resulted in a large number of nonresponses, as many settlers were not at home or sleeping when the researcher returned to collect the survey. To improve the response rate, the question was written into the survey as the last item in the remaining settlements.

7. While we may expect that some settlers would be hesitant about reporting criminal activities, a review of the distribution of reported vigilante behavior (Table 4.6) lends support to the validity of the item. As we would expect, settlements that have a long history of conflict with Arab

residents show very high participation in vigilantism (e.g., Elon Moreh, Beit Yatir, Shilo, or Ofra). Settlements more distant from Arab communities (Kfar Adumim, Karnei Shomron, and Sheve Shomron) show very low participation rates.

8. Only the most serious vigilante action noted was coded in the survey.

9. It should be noted that even isolated events had major impacts upon this small settlement movement. In the case of the Gush Emunim settlements, the most serious incident during the period of study was the stabbing to death of a Tekoah resident by teenagers from a nearby Arab village (Amrani, 1982b).

10. A number of settlers argued that they would prefer that the military authorities respond to Arab harassments, and settlers claimed that they often tried to elicit a military response before they reacted on their own. Some settlements were in areas with little or no visible military presence, and settlers argued that they were "forced" into the position of being their own policemen. Yet it should be kept in mind that vigilante actions were found in all but one of the settlements studied, many of which were located near to or even at army bases.

11. As settlers believed themselves to be acting within the law, these shooting incidents were not included as vigilante behaviors.

12. All Israeli men, after regular Army service and until the age of fifty-five, are required to serve reserve duty (forty-five days in 1983).

13. A number of settlers remarked that Arabs in the area were involved in fewer incidents during Ariel Sharon's tenure at the defense ministry. In their view, this was a period when the government acted forcefully against Arab unrest in the region.

14. As stoning incidents are not routinely reported in the Israeli press, it is virtually impossible to evaluate these settler claims.

15. In Shilo, for example, settlers were at first unwilling to allow data collection at the settlement because they feared researchers might be working with the government in its investigation of the shooting death of an Arab teenager. It is interesting to note in this regard that half of the men surveyed in this outpost did not answer the vigilante behavior item.

16. Among those indicted were founders of Ofra and Shilo, and at least one settler in this group participated in my qualitative interviews.

Chapter 5

1. For the distribution of this measure, see Table 4.3.

2. A weighted Ordinary Least Squares regression analysis technique is used. Weights are included to correct for the stratified sampling procedure used in data collection, and are based on estimates of the actual population of each settlement when the survey was conducted. (In this analysis there was no weighting for gender; it was not an important influence in the model and the sample size made the use of only one weighting dimension preferable.)

3. A statistical support for this argument is found in the fact that there is a weak though positive relationship ($r = +.14$) between settlement victimization and support for vigilantism when individual victimization scores are not controlled.

Multicolinearity problems provide an alternative explanation for this switch in variable effects in the multivariate model. Though multicollinearity usually results in insignificant parameters, it may at times cause a significant reverse in the influence of a measure (Gordon, 1968). When regressing the exogenous variables in the analysis upon settlement victimization, a diagnostic technique recommended by Tufte (1974), we find little evidence of multicollinearity (R^2 on $x = .49$).

4. Five of the settlements studied were located at an Israeli army base.

5. Given perceptions of Gush Emunim settlers as strongly messianic in orientation, it is interesting to note the large degree of variation in this measure. Sixteen and one-half percent of the settlers strongly agree with this item (see note c, Table 5.1), 25.4 percent agree, 25.5 percent had no opinion, 12.9 percent disagreed and 4.3 percent strongly disagreed. (Not stated = 15.4 percent).

6. The zero-order correlation between "group attitudes" and the residuals generated by the regression is not statistically significant.

7. In a regression model excluding "group attitudes," the effects of other independent variables generally become smaller. None of the measures that fail to achieve statistical significance in Table 5.2 become significant as a result of the exclusion of "group attitudes." In turn, the influence of "settlement victimization" is much larger in the full model (Table 5.2), and statistically not significant in the reduced model. These findings suggest that the regression including "group attitudes" is indeed a more stable and powerful one than that excluding the measure.

8. Jews whose origins lie in the Islamic countries are a generally disadvantaged group in Israeli society.

9. Because we examine the probability of vigilante behavior, a weighted logit regression is used. Ordinary Least Squares (OLS) regression may lead in this case to biased estimates of the true marginal probabilities associated with changes in the independent variables (Hanushek and Jackson, 1977; see also Nerlove and Press, 1973; McFadden, 1974). While the logistic form is appropriate for the problem we examine, the results are considerably more difficult to interpret than OLS estimates. Unlike the more common linear model, the logit estimates do not reflect a constant effect. Rather, they represent the change in the log of the odds associated with a unit change in the independent variable. Weights are included for gender and settlement size.

10. The logit response function of the probability of vigilante behavior (P of vigilante behavior $= 1/1 + e^{-xb}$) is thus approximated by setting the value of xb at 0 and then allowing the variable being estimated (b_i) to vary ($xb = 0 + b_i x_i$).

11. Due to a large number of missing values on this measure and the

necessity of using listwise deletion in the regression analysis estimated, "group attitudes" was used as a substitute when a score for individual attitudes was unavailable.

12. While the vigilante role may be expected of many in the settlements, I did not interview any settlers who stated that they had been formally sanctioned for not participating in vigilantism.

Chapter 6

1. This is illustrated by the extent to which settlers in the survey identified with the actions and ideas attributed to the Gush Emunim movement. Clearly, Gush Emunim was noted for its illegal settlement attempts and protests. In turn, almost three-quarters of the settlers supported most or all of the actions attributed to the Gush Emunim movement.

2. For settlers, the distinction between "passive" and "active" resistance was extremely important. In both cases there may be serious conflict with soldiers or the police. Yet in the case of "active" resistance, settlers saw themselves as resisting soldiers and not just standing by passively as they were removed or dispersed. For similar distinctions in evaluating American protest actions, see Hagan and Bernstein (1979).

3. It should be noted that the Hebrew word for violence—*Alimut*—may also mean powerful. It is used in Hebrew to refer to any type of violent conflict regardless of its intensity.

4. For many settlers these incidents represented traumatic experiences, regardless of the actual level of violence involved. The image of Israeli soldiers forcibly removing squatters from temporary encampments was not one Gush Emunim settlers were comfortable with. Nor was it an image these strongly nationalistic and Zionistic settlers wanted to give to their children.

5. Settlers were very sensitive about questions that alluded to potential settler violence in the future. They were especially annoyed at what they perceived as academic and press bias against the Gush Emunim movement. Because of this settler concern, and my desire not to have the survey as a whole rejected by respondents, this question was asked with the emphasis on passive resistance. Settlers who disagreed with this item, and thus disagreed that only passive resistance should be used, were seen as advocating active resistance to government attempts to restrict settlement.

6. This instability was the result of multicollinearity.

7. Social cohesion is measured through four items that relate to how settlers perceived their individual communities. Those who believed that settlers feel close to one another, that they will pull together in times of crisis, that their outposts are places where it is not hard to find friends, and that they themselves feel very much like they belong in their community were considered to be more strongly and positively linked to their settlement.

8. Settlers who strongly agree with both of these dimensions have much

more radical views on governmental deviance than those who base their definitions on only one of these norms. While the zero-order correlation between these variables is not extraordinarily high ($r = .24$, $p < .001$), their combination thus provides for a measure identifying those settlers who are most extreme in their attitudes toward deviance. It should be noted that separate regressions of each dimension produce weaker, though not theoretically variant, models than that presented in Table 6.9.

9. To correct for stratification biases and the overrepresentation of women in the sample, weights for both settlement size and sex were included in the regression analyses presented in Tables 6.9 and 6.10.

10. Those settlers who responded in the survey that the ideological commitment of a particular outpost played an important or predominant role in their settlement choice were given the mean score for the group attitudes measure.

11. Changes in all of the measures are small in the reduced model. None of the measures significant in Table 6.9 becomes insignificant, and only one measure (social cohesion) becomes significant. Importantly, the actual change in the size of b is small (from .063 to .083).

12. The criterion level is $P < .05$.

13. A potentially confounding problem exists if deviance is influencing attitudes toward community life. I used a reduced model to assess biases caused by these potential reciprocal effects. I found that the influence of social cohesion was greater in the context of a Two-Staged Least Squares regression analysis. The findings also suggest that other parameters in the model are not biased by these potential nonrecursive influences.

14. Settlements in which a majority of settlers either agreed or agreed strongly that only passive resistance could be used to combat government attempts to dismantle settlements were given a score of $+1$ ($N = 17$). All other settlements were given a score of -1.

15. Settlements were more clearly defined by their attitudes toward governmental deviance than by the types of sanctions they saw as appropriate. This is illustrated, for example, in Atzmona, which was established illegally in the Sinai before the withdrawal. This settlement was known as one of the most ideological of Gush Emunim outposts. Yet, these settlers were likely (according to the survey) to be passive in their reactions to the government. A similar example can be found in Elon Moreh, which is also known as an extremely ideological and radical settlement, yet shows in the survey relatively high support, as compared with other settlements, for passive resistance.

16. None of the measures significant in the full model loses significance in the reduced model. One measure, "Definitions of Deviance," becomes significant in the reduced model, though the change in its actual coefficient is relatively small (from $b = -.064$ to $b = -.079$).

17. See *Leviticus* 19:18. It should be noted that the rabbinical academies from which the Gush Emunim movement emerged have always supported the Zionist movement, even though it was dominated by secularists.

Chapter 7

1. There are similarities between my findings and those that place delinquency as a product of lower-class culture (e.g., Miller, 1958). At the same time, my argument does not assume that cultural norms encourage deviant behavior per se, but rather that violation of those norms in the larger society leads to deviant social reaction.

2. Black argues similarly that the neutralization perspective does not take into account the fact that offender condemnations of their victims "may be authentic" (1983:39).

3. My colleagues and I make a similar argument in reference to white-collar crime:

> Although much criminality is hedonistic, our criminal statutes criminalize acts that could hardly be said to be motivated by immediate and short term self-interest. In our sample, in addition to tax cheats we have tax protestors—persons who chose to express their unhappiness with our government by withholding the monies they owe. They, along with political terrorists or vigilantes, would be hard to explain in the simple terms put forth by a theory of ego gratification. (Wheeler et al., 1988:355)

4. In the case of the Jewish underground described in chapter 4, there was much disagreement among settlers over the legitimacy of the violence employed. Moreover, settlers involved in the underground appear not to have acted with direct community approval and support.

References

Abramov, S. Z. (1976). *Perpetual Dilemma: Jewish Religion in the Jewish State.* Rutherford, NJ: Fairleigh Dickinson.

Amann, P. H. (1983). "Vigilante Fascism: The Black Legion as an American Hybrid." *Comparative Study of Society and History* 25:490–524.

Amrani, I. (1982a, April 29). "The Government 'Encouraged' U.S. Anti-withdrawal Claims." *Jerusalem Post.*

Amrani, I. (1982b, August 4). "David's Dream." *Jerusalem Post.*

Andenaes, J. (1971). "The Moral or Educative Influence of Criminal Law." *Journal of Social Issues* 27:17–31.

Aronoff, M. J. (1984). "Gush Emunim: The Institutionalization of a Charismatic, Messianic, Religious-Political Revitalization Movement in Israel." *Religion and Politics, Political Anthropology,* vol. 3, New Brunswick, NJ: Transaction.

Avruch, K. (1979). "Gush Emunim: Politics, Religion, and Ideology in Israel." *Middle East Review* 11:26–31.

Bankston, W. B., R. L. St. Pierre, and H. D. Allen (1985). "Southern Culture and Patterns of Victim-Offender Relationships to Homicide: A Study of Primary and Nonprimary Homicide in Louisiana." *Sociological Spectrum* 5:197–211.

Baumgartner, M. P. (1984). "Social Control from Below." In D. Black, ed., *Toward a General Theory of Social Control* (vol. 1 Fundamentals), 303–45, New York: Academic Press.

Becker, H. (1963). *Outsiders: Studies in the Sociology of Deviance.* New York: Free Press.

Bell, J. (1977). *Terror Out of Zion: Irgun Zvai Leumi, LEHI, and the Palestine Underground, 1929–1949.* New York: St Martin's Press.

Benvenisti, M. (1982). *West Bank and Gaza Data Base Project* (Interim Report No. 1). Jerusalem.

Ben Zadoc, E. (1985). "The Limits of the Politics of Planning." In D. Newman, ed., *The Impact of Gush Emunim: Politics and Settlement in the West Bank.* New York: St. Martin's Press.

Black D. (1976). *The Behavior of Law.* New York: Academic Press.

Black D. (1983). "Crime as Social Control." *American Sociological Review* 43:34–45.

Black, D. (1984a). *Toward a General Theory of Social Control* (vol. 1, Fundamentals). New York: Academic Press.

Black, D. (1984b). *Toward a General Theory of Social Control* (vol. 2, Selected Problems). New York: Academic Press.

Black, D. (1984c). "Crime as Social Control." In D. Black, ed., *Toward a General Theory of Social Control* (vol. 2, Selected Problems), 1–27, New York: Academic Press.

Braithwaite, J. (1981). "The Myth of Social Class and Criminality Reconsidered." *American Sociological Review* 46:36–57.

Braithwaite, J. (1985). "White Collar Crime." *Annual Review of Sociology* 11:1–25.

Brilliant, J. (1975a, March 31). "20,000 March to Back Samaria Settlement." *Jerusalem Post.*

Brilliant, J. (1975b, December 5). "Samaria Settlement in Sixth Day." *Jerusalem Post.*

Brilliant, J. (1975c, December 4). "Settlers Affix Mezuzot to Sheds." *Jerusalem Post.*

Brilliant, J. (1975d, December 9). "Sebastia Settlers Can Stay in Army Camp." *Jerusalem Post.*

Brilliant, J. (1976, April 19). "Thousands March with Gush Emunim." *Jerusalem Post.*

Brilliant, J. (1977a, September 29). "Begin Approves Gush Emunim Settlements in Army Camps." *Jerusalem Post.*

Brilliant, J. (1977b, October 11). "Six Samaria Settlements Approved." *Jerusalem Post.*

Brilliant, J. (1977c, October 27). "Sharon: Don't Take Gush's Army Connections Literally." *Jerusalem Post.*

Brilliant, J. (1979, November 14). "Begin to Meet Gush on Elon Moreh Future." *Jerusalem Post.*

Billiant, J. (1982, March 5). "Evacuation of 3 More Settlements." *Jerusalem Post.*

Brown, R. M. (1971). "Legal and Behavioral Perspectives on American Vigilantism." *Perspectives in American History* 5:106–16.

Brown, R. M. (1975). *Strain of Violence: Historical Studies of American Violence and Vigilantism.* New York: Oxford University Press.

Brown, R. M. (1976). "The History of Vigilantism in America," in H. Rosenbaum and P. Sederberg, eds., *Vigilante Politics,* 79–109, Philadelphia: University of Pennsylvania.

Carroll, J., and F. Weaver (1986). "Shoplifters' Perceptions of Crime Opportunities: A Process-Tracing Study." In D. B. Cornish and R. V. Clarke, eds., *The Reasoning Criminal: Rational Choice Perspectives on Offending,* 19–38, New York: Springer-Verlag.

Caughey, J. W. (1957). "Their Majesties the Mob: Vigilantes Past and Present." *Pacific Historical Review* 26:217–34.

Clarke, R. V., and D. B. Cornish (1985). "Modeling Offenders' Decisions: A Framework for Research and Policy," In M. Tonray and N. Morris, eds., *Crime and Justice,* vol. 4, 147–85, Chicago: University of Chicago Press.

Chambliss, W. J. (1967). "Types of Deviance and the Effectiveness of Legal Sanctions." *Wisconsin Law Review* (Summer): 703–19.

Cohen, H. (1972). "Penal Law." In *Encyclopedia Judaica.* Keter: Jerusalem.
Coleman, J. W. (1987). "Toward an Integrated Theory of White Collar Crime." *American Journal of Sociology* 93:2, 406–39.
Cornish, D. B., and R. V. Clarke (1986a). *The Reasoning Criminal: Rational Choice Perspectives on Offending.* New York: Springer-Verlag.
Cornish, D. B., and R. V. Clarke (1986b). "Introduction." In D. B. Cornish and R. V. Clarke, eds., *The Reasoning Criminal: Rational Choice Perspectives on Offending,* 1–16, New York: Springer-Verlag.
Cornish, D. B., and R. V. Clarke (1987). "Understanding Crime Displacement: An Application of Rational Choice Theory." *Criminology* 4:933–47.
Coser, L. (1962). "Some Functions of Deviant Behavior and Normative Flexibility." *American Sociological Review* 48.
Davar (1983, August 19). "Interview with Avraham Achituv." *Davar.*
Deshen, S. (1978) "Two Trends in Israeli Orthodoxy." *Judaism* 27:397–409.
Deshen, S. (1982). "Israel Searching for Identity." In C. Caldarola, ed., *Religion and Societies.* Boston: Houghton Mifflin.
Diamond S. (1971). "The Rule of Law Versus the Order of Custom." *Social Research* 38:42–72.
Durkheim, Emile (1933), *The Division of Labor in Society.* New York: Free Press.
Ermann, M. D., and R. J. Lundman (1987). *Corporate and Governmental Deviance: Problems of Organizational Behavior in Contemporary Society.* New York: Oxford University Press.
Erikson, K. T. (1962). "Notes on the Sociology of Deviance." *Social Problems* 9:307–14.
Erikson, K. T. (1966). *Wayward Puritans: A Study in the Sociology of Deviance.* New York: John Wiley and Sons.
Farrell, W. F. (1977a, May 20). "Likud Follows Up Israeli Victory with Search for Coalition Allies." *New York Times.*
Farrell, W. F. (1977b, July 27). "West Bank Settlers Approved by Israel." *New York Times.*
Felson, M. (1987). "Routine Activities and Crime Prevention in the Developing Metropolis." *Criminology* 25:911–31.
Feeney, F. (1986). "Robbers as Decision-Makers." In D. B. Cornish and R. V. Clarke, eds., *The Reasoning Criminal: Rational Choice Perspectives on Offending,* 53–71, New York: Springer-Verlag.
Fisher, D. (1988, January 26). "Israel's Beatings Policy to Continue, Rabin Says." *Los Angeles Times.*
Friedman L. (1977). *Law and Society: An Introduction.* Englewood Cliffs, NJ: Prentice-Hall.
Friedman, T. (1985a, July 11). "Jewish Settlers are Convicted in Terror Cases." *New York Times.*
Friedman, T. (1985b, July 23). "Israeli Court Sentences 15 Jewish Terrorists." *New York Times.*
Friedman, T. (1987a, July 5) "My Neighbor, My Enemy." *New York Times Magazine.*

Friedman, T. (1987b, December 25). "Israel Strife: No Closer to a Solution." *New York Times.*

Gamson, W. (1975). *The Strategies of Social Protest.* Homewood, IL: The Dorsey Press.

Geis, G. (1984). "White Collar and Corporate Crime." In R. F. Meier, ed., *Major Forms of Crime*, 137–66, Beverly Hills, CA: Sage Publications.

Gerson, A. (1978). *Israel, The West Bank and International Law.* London: Frank Cass.

Gitlitz, J. S. and T. Rojas (1983). "Peasant Vigilante Committees in Northern Peru." *Journal of Latin American Studies* 15:163–97.

Glaser, D. (1979). "Economic and Sociocultural Variables Affecting Rates of Youth Unemployment, Delinquency and Crime." *Youth and Society* 11:53–82.

Glick, S. (1981). "The Tragedy of Gush Emunim." *Tradition* 19:112–21.

Goell, Y. (1981, January 30). "Gush Country." *Jerusalem Post.*

Goldberg, G., and E. Ben-Zadoc (1983). "Regionalism and Territorial Schism in the Making: Jewish Settlement in the Occupied Territories" (in Hebrew). *Series in State Government and International Relations* (21:69–94), Hebrew University.

Goodman, H. (1978, September 25). "Troops Morale 'Devastated' by Gush Emunim Clashes." *Jerusalem Post.*

Gordon, R. A. (1968). "Issues in Multiple Regression." *American Journal of Sociology* 73:592–616.

Gouldner, A. (1968). "The Sociologist as Partisan: Sociology and the Welfare State." *American Sociologist* 3:9–14.

Greenberg, D. (1981). *Crime and Capitalism: Readings in Marxist Criminology.* Palo Alto, CA: Mayfield Publishing.

Griffiths, J (1984). "The Division of Labor in Social Control." In D. Black, ed., *Toward a General Theory of Social Control* (vol. 1, Fundamentals), 37–70, New York: Academic Press.

Gurr, T. (1970). *Why Men Rebel.* Princeton, NJ: Princeton University Press.

Gush Emunim (1975). "Gush Emunim: Newsletter" (in Hebrew). *Gush Emunim.* Jerusalem.

HaAretz (1984, June 20). "Results of Pori Research Organization Survey." *HaAretz.*

Hagan, J., and I. N. Bernstein (1979). "Conflict in Context: The Sanctioning of Draft Registers, 1963–76." *Social Problems* 27:109–22.

Hagan, J., and P. Parker (1985). "White Collar Crime and Punishment: The Class Structure and Legal Sanctioning of Securities Violations." *American Sociological Review* 50: 302–16.

Hanushek, E., and J. Jackson (1977). *Statistical Methods for Social Scientists.* New York: Academic Press.

Hirschi, T. (1969). *Causes of Delinquency.* Berkeley: University of California Press.

Hirschi, T., and M. Gottfredson (1987). "Causes of White Collar Crime." *Criminology* 25: 949–74.

Honig, S. (1974, October 21). *Jerusalem Post.*

Horowitz, I. L., and M. Leibowitz (1968). "Social Deviance and Political Marginality: Towards a Redefinition of the Relationship Between Sociology and Politics." *Social Problems* 15:280–96.

Horowitz, I. L. (1987). "Disenthralling Sociology." *Society* (January/ February), 49–55.

Israel Central Bureau of Statistics (1982). *Statistical Abstract of Israel.* Jerusalem: Central Bureau of Statistics.

Issac, R. J. (1976). *Israel Divided.* Baltimore, MD: Johns Hopkins University Press.

Jerusalem Post (1975, March 20). "Sabastia Settlers Evicted with Force on Both Sides."

Jerusalem Post (1976, March 29). "Settle West Bank, Say Kibbutz, Moshav Members."

Jerusalem Post (1977a, June 5).

Jerusalem Post (1977b, September 16). "Rabbi Kook Calls on Gush Emunim to Heed Government."

Jerusalem Post (1978, September 29). "Gush Squatters Evicted by Force."

Jerusalem Post (1980, February 13). "Britain's Chief Rabbi Backs Palestine State."

Jerusalem Post (1981, March 17). "25,000 March in Protest Over Sinai."

Johnson, J. M., and J. D. Douglas (1978). *Crime at the Top: Deviance in Business and the Professions.* Philadelphia: J. B. Lippincott.

Karp, J. (1983). "Investigation of Suspicions against Israelis in Judea and Samaria" (in Hebrew). Misrad HaMishpatim: State of Israel.

Katz, E., and M. Gurevitch (1976). *The Secularization of Leisure: Culture and Communication in Israel.* Cambridge: Harvard University Press.

Katz, J. (1980). "The Social Movement against White Collar Crime." *Criminology Review Yearbook,* Vol. 2, 161–184. Beverly Hills, CA: Sage Publications.

Kitsuse, J. I. (1962). "Societal Reaction to Deviant Behavior: Problems of Theory and Method." *Social Problems* 28:1–13.

Kitsuse, J. I., and A. J. Cicoural (1963). "A Note on the Use of Official Statistics." *Social Problems* 11: 131–39.

Kitsuse, J. I. (1980). "Coming Out All Over: Deviants and the Politics of Social Problems." *Social Problems* 28:1–13.

Kohn, M. (1976a, August 6). "The Roots Go Back to the 'Fifties.' " *Jerusalem Post.*

Kohn M. (1976b, August 8). "The NRP and the Gush." *Jerusalem Post.*

Kooistra, P. G. (1985). "What is Political Crime?" *Criminal Justice Abstracts,* 17, no. 1.

Kreml, W. P. (1976). "The Vigilante Personality." In H. Rosenbaum and P. Sederberg, eds., *Vigilante Politics,* 45–63. Philadelphia: University of Pennsylvania Press.

Landau, D. (1976). "Kaddum Debate Looms: Begin Sounds Warning." *Jerusalem Post.*

Lauderdale, P. (1976). "Deviance and Moral Boundaries." *American Sociological Review* 41: 660–76.

Lauderdale, P. (1980). *A Political Analysis of Deviance.* Minneapolis: University of Minnesota Press.

Lebow, R. (1976). "Vigilantism in Northern Ireland." In H. Rosenbaum and P. Sederberg, eds., *Vigilante Politics,* 234–258. Philadelphia: University of Pennsylvania Press.

Lesch, A. M. (1980). *Political Perceptions of the Palestinians on the West Bank and Gaza Strip.* Washington, D.C.: The Middle East Institute.

Lewis, A. (1984). "Ethnic Politics and the Foreign Policy Debate in Israel." *Political Anthropology* 4.

Liazos, A. (1972). "The Poverty of the Sociology of Deviance: Nuts, Sluts and Preverts." *Social Problems* 20:103–20.

Little, C. B., and C. P. Sheffield (1983). "Frontiers and Criminal Justice: English Private Prosecution Societies and American Vigilantism in the Eighteenth and Nineteenth Centuries." *American Sociological Review* 48:796–808.

Lustick, I. (1981). "Israel and the West Bank after Elon Moreh: The Mechanics of DeFacto Annexation." *Middle East Journal* 35:957–77.

Lustick I. (1987). "Israel's Dangerous Fundamentalists." *Foreign Policy* (November), 118–39.

Miller, W. B. (1958). "Lower Class Culture as a Generating Milieu of Gang Delinquency." *Journal of Social Issues* 14:5–19.

Mann, K. (1985). *Defending White Collar Crime: A Portrait of Attorneys at Work.* New Haven: Yale University Press.

Ma'Oz, M. (1984). *Palestinian Leadership on the West Bank.* London: F. Cass.

McFadden, D. (1974). "Conditional Logit Analysis of Qualitative Choice and Behavior." In P. Zarembka, ed., *Frontiers in Econometrics.* New York: Academic Press.

Merton, R. K. (1938). "Social Structure and Anomie." *American Sociological Review* 3:672–82.

Michalowski, R. J. (1981). "Conflict, Radical, and Critical Approaches to Criminology." In I. L. Barak-Glantz and C. R. Huff, eds., *The Mad, The Bad and the Different,* 39–52. Lexington, MA: Lexington Books.

Nerlove, M., and S. J. Press (1973). *Univariate and Multivariate Loglinear and Logistic Models.* Santa Monica, CA: Rand Corporation.

Newman, D. (1982). "Jewish Settlement in the West Bank: The Role of Gush Emunim." *Occasional Papers,* no. 16. University of Durham Center for Middle Eastern and Islamic Studies.

Newman, D. (1985a). "Spatial Structures and Ideological Change in the West Bank." In D. Newman, ed., *The Impact of Gush Emunim,* 172–81. New York: St. Martin's Press.

Newman, D. (1985b). *The Impact of Gush Emunim.* New York: St. Martin's Press.

New York Times (1985, May 22). "Furor Grows in Israel Over Jailed Jews."

Odea, J. (1976). "Gush Emunim: Roots and Ambiguities: The Perspective of the Sociology of Religion." *Forum* 2:39–50.

Olson, M. (1965). *The Logic of Collective Action.* Cambridge: Harvard University Press.

Parsons, T. (1951). *The Social System.* Toronto: Collier-MacMillan.

Piven, F. F. (1981). "Deviant Behavior and the Remaking of the World." *Social Problems* 28:490–508.

Potholm, C. P. (1976). "Comparative Vigilantism: The United States and South Africa." In H. Rosenbaum and P. Sederberg, eds., *Vigilante Politics*, 175–93, Philadelphia: University of Pennsylvania Press.

Quinney, R. (1973). *Critique of Legal Order: Crime Control in Capitalist Society.* Boston: Little, Brown.

Quinney, R. (1977). *Class, State, and Crime.* New York: David McKay.

Raanan, Z. (1981). *Gush Emunim* (in Hebrew). Tel Aviv: Workers Press.

Rabinowitz, A. (1978a, September 20). "Gush Settlers Eviction Ordered by Cabinet." *Jerusalem Post.*

Rabinowitz, A. (1978b, September 28). "Subdued Settlers Protest at Knesset." *Jerusalem Post.*

Reich, W. (1984). *A Stranger in My House: Jews and Arabs in the West Bank.* New York: Holt, Rinehart and Winston.

Reiss, A. J., Jr. (1961). "The Social Integration of Queers and Peers." *Social Problems* 9:102–20.

Reiss, A. J., Jr. (1966). "The Study of Deviant Behavior: Where the Action Is." *Ohio Valley Sociologist* 25:308–23.

Richardson, D. (1979, October 23). "Government Won't Sidestep Court Ruling on Elon Moreh; Gush Settlers Must Leave Within a Month." *Jerusalem Post.*

Rinott, C. (1972). "Israel, State of: Education and Science." In *Encyclopaedia Judaica.* Jerusalem: Keter Publishing House.

Rock, P. (1974). "The Sociology of Deviancy and Conceptions of Moral Order." *British Journal of Criminology* 14:139–49.

Rosenbaum, J. H., and P. C. Sederberg (1974). "Vigilantism: An Analysis of Establishment Violence." *Comparative Politics* 6:541–70.

Rosenbaum, J. H., and P. C. Sederberg (1976). "Vigilantism: An Analysis of Establishment Violence." In H. Rosenbaum and P. Sederberg, eds., *Vigilante Politics*, 3–29. Philadelphia: University of Pennsylvania Press.

Rubinstein, D. (1982). *On the Lord's Side: Gush Emunim* (in Hebrew). Tel Aviv: Workers Press.

Sagarin, E. (1975). *Deviants and Deviance: An Introduction to the Study of Disvalued People and Behavior.* New York: Praeger Publishers.

Sagarin, E. (1985). "Positive Deviance: An Oxymoron." *Deviant Behavior* 6:169–81.

SAS (1982). *SAS User's Guide.* Cary, NC: SAS Institute.

Schafer, S. (1971). "The Political Criminal." *Journal of Criminal Law, Criminology and Police Science* 62:380–87.

Schnall, D. J. (1977). "Gush Emunim: Messianic Dissent and Israeli Politics." *Judaism* 26:148–60.

Schnall, D. (1985). "An Impact Assessment." In D. Newman, ed., *The Impact of Gush Emunim*, 13–26. New York: St. Martin's Press.

Schur, E. M. (1980). *The Politics of Deviance: Stigma Contests and the Uses of Power*. Englewood Cliffs, NJ: Prentice-Hall.

Schwartz, R. (1954). "Social Factors in the Development of Legal Control: A Case Study of Two Israeli Settlements." *Yale Law Journal* 63:471–91.

Scully, D., and J. Marolla (1985). " 'Riding the Bull at Gilley's': Convicted Rapists Describe the Rewards of Rape." *Social Problems* 32:251–63.

Sederberg, P. (1978). "The Phenomenology of Vigilantism in Contemporary America." *International Journal of Terrorism* 1:287–303.

Shafir, G. (1983). "Changing Nationalism and Israel's Open Frontier on the West Bank." Unpublished Paper, Tel Aviv University, Department of Sociology.

Shafir, G. (1985). "Institutional and Spontaneous Settlement Drives: Did Gush Emunim Make a Difference?" In D. Newman, ed., *The Impact of Gush Emunim*, 153–71. New York: St Martin's Press.

Shapiro, A. (1983, June 14). "The Rule of Law and the West Bank." *Jerusalem Post*.

Shapiro, S. (1984). *Wayward Capitalists: Target of the Securities and Exchange Commission*. New Haven: Yale University Press.

Shilhav, Y. (1985). "Interpretation and Misinterpretation of Jewish Territorialism" In D. Newman, ed., *The Impact of Gush Emunim*, 111–24, New York: St. Martin's Press.

Shipler, D. (1982, March 28). "The West Bank Occupation Now Resembles Annexation." *New York Times*.

Shipler, D. (1984a, February 6). "Israelis Declare Curb on Violence on West Bank and the Gaza Strip." *New York Times*.

Shipler, D. (1984b, February 8). "Israelis Admit Laxity on Offenses by Settlers." *New York Times*.

Shipler, D. (1984c, May 9). "Anti-Arab Violence Sets Off Debate in Israel." *New York Times*.

Shipler, D. (1984d, June 8). "Some Support Emerging in Settlements for Israelis Charged as Terrorists." *New York Times*.

Shipler D. (1987). *Arab and Jew: Wounded Spirits in the Promised Land*. New York: Penguin Books.

Shotland, R. L. (1976). "Spontaneous Vigilantes." *Society* 13(3), 30–32.

Skolnick, J. H. (1969). *The Politics of Protest*. New York: Ballantine Books.

Smelser, N. (1962). *Theory of Collective Behavior*. New York: Free Press.

Solovechik, J. (1975, September 5). Interview. *Maariv*.

Spector, M. (1976). "Labelling Theory in Social Problems: A Young Journal Launches a New Theory." *Social Problems* 24:68–75.

Sprinzak, E. (1977). "Extreme Politics in Israel." *Jerusalem Quarterly* 5: 36–46.

Sprinzak, E. (1981). "Gush Emunim: The Tip of the Iceberg." *Jerusalem Quarterly* 21:28–47.

Stark, R. (1987). "Deviant Places: A Theory of the Ecology of Crime." *Criminology* 25:893–910.

Stone, T. (1979). "The Mounties as Vigilantes: Perceptions of Community and the Transformation of Law in the Yukon, 1885–1897." *Law and Society Review* 14:83–114.

Sutherland, E. H., and D. R. Cressey (1960). *Principles of Criminology*, 6th ed., Philadelphia: J. B. Lippincott.

Sykes, G. (1965). *The Society of Captives*. New York: Atheneum.

Sykes, G., and D. Matza (1957). "Techniques of Neutralization: A Theory of Delinquency." *American Sociological Review* 22:664–70.

Tal, U. (1976). "The Nationalism of Gush Emunim in Historical Perspective." *Forum* 36:11–14.

Taylor, I., P. Warton, and J. Young (1973). *The New Criminology: For a Social Theory of Deviance*. New York: Harper and Row.

Thrasher, F. M. (1927). *The Gang*. Chicago: University of Chicago Press.

Tittle, C. R., W. J. Villemez, and D. Smith (1978). "The Myth of Social Class and Criminality." *American Sociological Review* 43:643–56.

Tucker, W. (1985). *Vigilante: The Backlash Against Crime in America*. New York: Stein and Day Publishers.

Tufte, E. R. (1974). *Data Analysis for Politics and Policy*. Englewood Cliffs, NJ: Prentice-Hall.

Turk, A. T. (1982). *Political Criminality: The Defiance and Defense of Authority*. Beverly Hills, CA: Sage Publications.

Vaughan, D. (1983). *Controlling Unlawful Organizational Behavior: Social Structure and Corporate Misconduct*. Chicago: University of Chicago Press.

Walsh, D. (1986). "Victim Selection Procedures Among Economic Criminals: The Rational Choice Perspective." In D. B. Cornish and R. V. Clarke, eds., *The Reasoning Criminal: Rational Choice Perspectives on Offending*, 39–52, New York: Springer-Verlag.

Wallfish, A. (1975, December 4). "Knesset to Hold Full-Dress Debate on Samaria." *Jerusalem Post*.

Wallfish, A. (1979a, January 5). "Begin Pledges More Settlements, But Says Government Will Set Timetable." *Jerusalem Post*.

Wallfish, A. (1979b, October 24). "Begin is Seeking New Site for Elon Moreh." *Jerusalem Post*.

Warton, P. (1973). "The Case of the Weathermen: Social Reaction and Radical Commitment." *Mens en Maatschapp* 48:12–34.

Waxman, C. (1975). "Political and Social Attitudes of Americans Among the Settlers in the Territories." In D. Newman, ed., *The Impact of Gush Emunim*, 200–220, New York: St. Martin's Press.

Weisburd, D., E. Waring, and S. Wheeler (1987). "Examining Opportunity Structures in White Collar Crime." American Society of Criminology Meetings. Montreal, Canada.

Weissbrod, L. (1982). "Gush Emunim Ideology: From Religious Doctrine to Political Action." *Middle East Studies* 18:265–75.

Weissbrod L. (1984). "Protest and Dissidence in Israel." In M. J. Aronoff, ed., *Cross Currents in Israeli Culture and Politics, Political Anthropology* 4:51–68, New Brunswick, NJ: Transaction Books.

Weizman, E. (1981). *The Battle for Peace.* New York: Bantam Books.

Weller, L. (1974). *Sociology in Israel.* Westport, CT: Greenwood Press.

Wheeler, S. (1961). "Role Conflict in Correctional Communities." In Donald R. Cressey, ed., *The Prison: Studies in Institutional and Organizational Change.* New York: Holt, Rinehart and Winston.

Wheeler, S., and M. Rothman (1982). "The Organization as Weapon in White Collar Crime." *Michigan Law Review* 80:1403–26.

Wheeler, S., D. Weisburd, E. Waring, and N. Bode (1988). "White Collar Crime and Criminals." *American Criminal Law Review* 25:331–357.

Wilkins, L. T. (1965). *Social Deviance.* Englewood Cliffs, NJ: Prentice-Hall.

Williams, R. (1962). *American Society.* New York: Alfred A. Knopf.

Wilson, J. Q., and R. J. Herrnstein (1985). *Crime and Human Nature.* New York: Simon and Schuster.

Yadlin, A. (1972). "Israel, State of: Youth Movements." In *Encyclopaedia Judaica* 9:976–82.

Zinger, Z. 1972). "Kook, Abraham Isaac (1865–1935)." In *Encyclopaedia Judaica* 10:1182–87.

Name Index

Subject Index